The Crowd is Untruth

American University Studies

Series V
Philosophy

Vol. 176

PETER LANG
New York • Washington, D.C./Baltimore
Bern • Frankfurt am Main • Berlin • Vienna • Paris

Howard N. Tuttle

The Crowd is Untruth

The Existential Critique of Mass Society in the Thought of Kierkegaard, Nietzsche, Heidegger, and Ortega y Gasset

PETER LANG
New York • Washington, D.C./Baltimore
Bern • Frankfurt am Main • Berlin • Vienna • Paris

Library of Congress Cataloging-in-Publication Data

Tuttle, Howard N. (Howard Nelson)
The crowd is untruth: the existential critique of mass society in the thought of
Kierkegaard, Nietzsche, Heidegger, and Ortega y Gasset/ Howard N. Tuttle.
p. cm. — (American university studies. Series V, Philosophy; vol. 176)
Includes bibliographical references.
1. Existentialism. 2. Mass society. 3. Kierkegaard, Søren, 1813–1855.
4. Nietzsche, Friedrich Wilhelm, 1844–1900. 5. Heidegger, Martin, 1889–
1976. 6. Ortega y Gasset, José, 1883–1955. I. Title. II. Series.
B819.T88   142'.78–dc20   95-16841
ISBN 0-8204-2866-3
ISSN 0739-6392

Die Deutsche Bibliothek-CIP-Einheitsaufnahme

Tuttle, Howard N.:
The crowd is untruth: the existential critique of mass society in the thought of
Kierkegaard, Nietzsche, Heidegger, and Ortega y Gasset/ Howard N. Tuttle.
–New York; Washington, D.C./Baltimore; Bern; Frankfurt am Main; Berlin;
Vienna; Paris: Lang.
(American university studies: Ser. 5, Philosophy; Vol. 176)
ISBN 0-8204-2866-3
NE: American university studies/ 05

Excerpts from *Fear and Trembling and The Sickness unto Death* by
Kierkegaard, translated by Walter Lowrie. Princeton: Princeton University
Press, 1954. Reprinted by permission of Princeton University Press.

The paper in this book meets the guidelines for permanence and durability
of the Committee on Production Guidelines for Book Longevity
of the Council of Library Resources.

Printed in the United States of America.

For my son

Carl Emerson Tuttle

"But, in fact, we are all collective beings, let us place ourselves as we may. For how little have we, and are we, that we can strictly call our own property . . . But many good men do not comprehend that; and they grope in darkness for half a life, with their dreams of originality."

Goethe
Conversations with Eckermann

"'*The crowd*' is essentially what I am aiming my polemical arrow at; and it was Socrates who taught me to do so. I want people to sit up and take notice, to prevent them from idling away and wasting their lives."

Kierkegaard
Journals, 5979

Table of Contents

? How can the evolution of the individual in existentialism benefit/evolve the masses in a way that Christianity doesn't?

Preface

A specter is haunting our era, a specter that current philosophical thinking has tended to ignore or tolerate as normal. This specter is not Marx's specter of communism, nor is it an emerging and muscular capitalism, nor any political left or right, but a shade that can materialize as any of these. Its name is the mass. This work is intended as a delineation and critique of this phenomenon through the writings of four select philosophers who have significantly dealt with this subject in their respective philosophies: Kierkegaard, Nietzsche, Heidegger, and Ortega y Gasset. While other recent thinkers have also addressed this topic, for example Emerson, Thoreau, Unamuno, Berdyaev, Marcel, Jaspers, Camus and Marcuse, our selected four have integrated the event of the mass into the very doctrinal structure of their philosophies. Also, in the opinion of the author, they have revealed the most essential dimensions of recent philosophical thought on the subject. But what do we mean by the mass? Tentatively we shall indicate by this term that collective population which is contrasted with specific social classes or groups per se. The mass is any multitude which is seen dominantly as number, quantity, or externality, as opposed to individual quality or internality. For our four thinkers this mass is not simply another perspective upon an irksome modernism which we may applaud or condemn. Rather, the phenomenon's conceptualization and evaluation has become for them a crucial element in their philosophical concerns. These thinkers see the mass not only as something sociologically decisive, but as a significant philosophical issue that requires moral clarification and philosophical identification. In other words, the mass is a constituent of our human condition, a possibility of human being in general. Finally, for our four thinkers the mass is integrally related to or identified with modern nihilism, a doctrine which denies any objective or real ground for truth or moral values.

These four understood the mass and its purported nihilism as something recent and novel in human history, phenomena which arose in the mid-nineteenth century, together with the increase of liberal democracy, scientific experiment, and industrialism; the mass and nihilism have continued through our own century and display portents for the twenty-first century. Our thinkers would distinguish the mass from the multitudes, or what Socrates called the "many." The many, the majority, have been with us since recorded history, appearing as large populations or collectives. In the Ancient Roman world Seneca bewailed the multitude who thronged the arenas to enjoy the torture and death of men and animals. The *New Testament* recognized a "world system," a multitude composed of many nations whose institutions and practices were pernicious to the life of the spirit. Both Montaigne and Goethe noted the rise of large groups of indifferent quality who inaugurated the printing press, nationalism, and popular culture. In these examples we have the ancient phenomenon of the multitude or the "many." But the mass in our sense is an advent of the mid-nineteenth century, and as a purely philosophical notion it was first conceptualized by the theologian and philosopher Søren Kierkegaard (1813-1855). Philosophically, he was the first to discern not only the genesis of the masses in nineteenth century Europe, but also the historical developments through which this event was made possible; he was the first theorist of the secular leveling that characterizes modern massification; and he was the first to perceive the immense significance of this event for the individual. He maintained, especially in his *Two Ages*, that no theory of the contemporary individual is possible without a consideration of mass leveling. This also means that the contemporary understanding of Christianity, culture, psychology, and government cannot be academically complete without reference to the "crowd" or "public," Kierkegaard's names for the mass as he understood it. It was Kierkegaard who said, "The crowd is untruth," and his expression refers not so much to an ignorance in Socrates' sense, but to the fact that the very existence of the crowd causes the individual to forget or misappre-

(faults of Christianity)
since this religion
groups the individuals
into a massive singular
body

Next page

Existentialism forces
the individual to think &
act upon an individual
basis, thus enhancing the
intellect of the masses

hend his or her possibilities as an individual. Also the mass fosters in the individual conformity, irresponsibility, and despair. Here the mass becomes the enemy of self-transcendence, because it tends to freeze the individual in the actualities of his or her present. In other words, the crowd is "untruth" because it convinces us of our personal unfreedom and relative unimportance. It convinces us that we are only significant to the extent that we share in the status of a crowd.

From one point of view, Kierkegaard's thought can be seen as the thinking individual's protest against the influence of Hegel on European thought and Christian culture. Kierkegaard believed that Hegel's rationalism had promoted the assumption that the individual and society must be understood as conceptual universals at the expense of concrete human existence. But for Kierkegaard and the philosophers we examine, it is only the individual subject who most fully embodies the real. The actualities of existence belong primarily to the individual, and both Hegelianism and official state Christianity had forgotten this, according to Kierkegaard. Kierkegaard's mission was to shake us into awareness of this in a Christian context. He did this by addressing what he considered the primary affliction of modernism, the collapse of individual existence as the most authentic aspect of Being. Whereas Hegel had asked how society was possible, and had conceptualized a framework in which authentic human existence was only possible as social existence, Kierkegaard asked how personal existence is possible. To the consternation of both academic and church leaders, Kierkegaard protested that both freedom and individuation had no clearly defined import in the Hegelian system, and that the individual could not be left, as Hegel's system would have it, to be unfolded only through socialization and history. Both Kierkegaard and Nietzsche believed that Hegelianism promoted conceptual and moral massification.

Kierkegaard, then, was the first to undertake a comprehensive critique of his age, with the implication that his findings would be applicable to the next century. Nietzsche, following Kierkegaard, would do the same. Both thinkers are seen today as dealing with contemporary issues, and much current thought derives from their assertions that the central issue of modernism is the question of the quality of our existence as individuals. Both Kierkegaard and Nietzsche believed the tendency of the future was to equality and leveling, and their thinking would influence writers such as Albert Camus, who saw our contemporary condition in terms of the pridefulness of the masses, who have attempted a secular duplication of God through the apotheosis of history and society. This tendency, Camus thought, could be traced to Rousseau, Hegel, and Marx, three thinkers who all anticipated the amalgamation of individual existence with the processes of politics, bureaucracy, and economics. For the Christian Kierkegaard, this condition or amalgamation can only be counteracted, if at all, through transcendent commitment and individuation.

God's failure equated to the "death" non existence of God in the minds of the new leading to despair & inactivity

For Nietzsche, the founder of atheistic existentialism, the root of massification in the Western world in fact results from our implicit recognition of the failure of divine agency, the death of God. The masses, for Nietzsche, are those who exist through the inauthentic secular substitutes for Christian faith. In Nietzsche, the resultant problem of nihilism comes to be the essential fact of modernity, a fact from which the existence of the masses cannot be separated. For Nietzsche it is not religious but secular self-transcendence that presents itself as the means of individuation. The human being becomes here the product of self-making, and the great enemy of Nietzsche's self-fabricational transcendence remains the nihilism of the inert and superfluous mass. This massification can be overcome, if at all, only by the self-transcending human fabrication of the overman. *Evolution of members of masses into creatively productive indiv*

For both Heidegger and Ortega y Gasset, the response to massification need not possess a religious dimension. For them massification is the result of the very social nature of the human being. For them the individual and the mass exhibit an isomorphic relation to each other in that the individual possesses as part of his or her makeup the possibility to slide from an individuated to a mass state, which Heidegger called *das Man* and Ortega the *hombre masa*. This mass status is a constant possibility of our being. Also, both thinkers understood massification in close relationship to industrial technology. While this element plays a small role in the thought of Kierkegaard and

Nietzsche, in both Heidegger and Ortega y Gasset this issue comes to the forefront of their analysis of the mass. Kierkegaard and Nietzsche were not interested in technology, economics, or sociology as such; instead, it was individuals they aimed at polemically, in the attempt to make them aware of the possibility to become what they are, apart from their collective existence. Heidegger retained Kierkegaard's concern that individual existence and commitment receive priority over collective relations, but Heidegger understood individual existence under the overarching issue of the question of the meaning of Being, and it is this ontological emphasis which distinguishes him from Kierkegaard.

In the thought of Ortega y Gasset, we have a primary concern for human life as radical reality. In this sense Ortega shares Heidegger's orientation to fundamental ontology. Ortega's position that the human being is an individuated self-creation in historical time finds similar expression in the three other thinkers; and for all of them the modern masses represent an aberration from the authentic self-making possibilities of humanity. For these thinkers contemporary human existence is a sort of pseudo or inauthentic life. The function of philosophy is to identify those attitudes and commitments that best induce our self-development out of the mass. Human life requires a return to concrete individual existence, and the analysis of how our four thinkers conceptualized this existence in the face of the mass is the theme to which we must now turn.

PART ONE

SØREN KIERKEGAARD

Chapter One

The Origin of Kierkegaard's Problem of the Mass and the Individual

(A) The Enlightenment

The secular traditions of European history against which Kierkegaard was to react were the eighteenth century Enlightenment and the rise of mass society in the nineteenth century. Both of these traditions were to become part of his philosophical and theological problematics, and both were his enemies. The Enlightenment can be characterized as the attempt to advance to a secular public the ideas and attitudes of an educated minority who were grounded in the empiricism of Bacon and Locke. This minority was largely composed of *philosophes*, who were popularizers and propagandists of ideas rather than philosophers as such. It was through the efforts of such men as Voltaire, Diderot, and Condorcet that reason became enthroned in the Enlightenment as the authentic sovereign of individual and historical life. These *philosophes* had it as their end to "enlighten" society through the formation of an ideal secular humanity, with its attendant institutions. The French "enlighteners" were sometimes less constructive than radical, and they often sought the destruction of the royal abuse of kingly power and the feudal structures of culture and religion. The primary French contribution to this end was the *Encyclopedie ou Dictionaire raisonné des sciences, arts et metiers*, 1751-1772, in twenty-eight volumes, edited by Diderot, D'Alembert, Helvetius, and Holbach. Their "cult of reason" was developed partly out of disaffection with the Reformation and with revealed religion generally. They maintained an impassioned zeal for the construction, through reason, education, and social planning, of an ideal man and an ideal society free from the moral, religious, and material limits of the old regime.

Part of what underlay these revolutionary ideals was the assumption that the social and psychological sciences (what John Stuart Mill called the "moral sciences") could be used in the service of reconstructing secular humanity. These "moral sciences" were held to possess a rational formulation based in the rise of the mathematical sciences of the prior seventeenth century. Economics, psychology, and history were believed to possess the general validity of the natural sciences as they had been formulated in the seventeenth century by Copernicus, Kepler, Galileo, and Newton. These earlier scientists had assumed that the world was composed of material bodies and their motions in space. Such bodies and motions could be given mathematical expression as the "laws of nature," and these laws implied that when physical phenomena were subsumed under them, they would express the same necessity that axioms bear to theorems. It was also assumed that nature could only be comprehended in terms of certain "primary qualities," i.e., such quantifiable and material elements as weight, velocity, figure, extension, position, magnitude, and number. These were for them the "primary qualities" without which nature could not exist as she is "in herself." Also, such qualities were considered the very essence of matter, because they composed the external world as it is in itself quite apart from any perceptual or subjective appearance it might have to the ordinary observer. On the other hand, the ordinary sense-characteristics of physical things, such as colors, smells, tastes, and feelings, were termed the "secondary qualities" of nature. They were designated as "secondary" in the sense that they were believed to be merely the subjective, mediated appearance of nature as she is in her primary state. But the founders of mathematical science reserved the designation "reality" for only the primary qualities.

It was in René Descartes (1596-1650) that Europe felt the impact of these premises for the human studies and theology. In his *Discourse on Method* and *Meditations of First Philosophy*, Descartes (and the subsequent rationalistic tradition) assumed that the non-scientific studies could never possess adequate knowledge. Valid inquiry was to be restricted to the mathematical comprehension of nature in its primary status. This implied that the secondary, qualitative states of human experience, the states described by the humanities and theology, would be assigned to the realms of illusion and subjectivity. These subjects simply could not be comprehended by the quantitative-mathematical methods of the sciences without eliminating what human beings and their works are about, i.e., ideas, volitions, feelings, first-person states, sense data, cultural artifacts and symbolizations and records, institutions, the arts, religion, and language. Because Descartes' monomethodology would not accommodate these human-expression materials, they were relegated to a sub-rational and sub-real status in which they would remain until the nineteenth century. For the Enlightenment thinkers of the eighteenth century, then, eager to be included in the scientific, rationalist camp, Isaac Newton (1642-1727) was the model for both method and subject-matter; the human world could be reduced to laws, quantities, experiments which could result in prescriptions for a new society. By searching for laws of human behavior and by reconstructing society according to the laws of nature, they could create an Enlightenment-based social science of secular "progress" (with all the liberal norms developed in the nineteenth century), whereby society could save humanity. For example, Adam Smith advocated that economics should be allowed to proceed according to its own laws and assumptions and natural tendencies. But the Enlightenment "scientism" was to result in undermining our actual, lived existence, which we do not experience externally. Our internal, lived experience tended to be relegated to a subjective or illusory status, so that questions of meaning or the final end of human existence became ignored.

Then Hegel would bring to these materials a new competence in methodology and rational explication through his absolute idealism. We will see a delineation of Hegel's competence in Section E, for it was from Hegel that Kierkegaard received the philosophy and method through which he would come to understand the status of the individual as a historical composition of ideal universalities. Yet these universalities seemed to Kierkegaard to ignore the actual condition of our personal nature and destiny in the mid-nineteenth century, just as the scientific mentality had ignored them in the seventeenth and eighteenth. Kierkegaard's thought would therefore become anti-Hegelian. Neither science nor Hegel could reveal the reality of our condition or the principles which justify the individual before the Infinite.

(B) Rousseau's Assumptions

From the moral and social influences that the Enlightenment would exert on Kierkegaard's mid-nineteenth century, none would surpass in potency those exerted by the eighteenth century thinker Jean-Jacques Rousseau (1712-1778). Rousseau had attempted to revive the doctrine of the historical origin of democratic ideals from a more natural and rational "state of nature." He had opposed to the society of his time the primitive virtues and strengths which he believed to reside in this "state of nature." Modernity was for Rousseau a fall from the original happiness and authenticity of the earlier state into the moral and social decadence of his own time. In the prior natural state human beings had lived only for the satisfaction of their primary needs, and in their natural equality they exercised their free will to the end of their self-perfection.

But with the coming of private property there grew up an artificial division in the natural polity between the rich and the poor. This division was made permanent by the legal system and the assumptions of social inequality. While individuals in the state of nature were basically moral beings for Rousseau, they have subsequently become corrupted through their deviation from the more natural conditions of the state of nature. The purpose of all political society is to rectify this fall from the uncorrupted conditions of our earlier natural state. One means to this end is to insure that all legitimate political society be grounded in the consent of the governed. But this consent requires for its permanence a social contract, an agreement between individuals that those who seek a new political order must form a society without anarchy or the coercion of the individual by the group. To insure this condition Rousseau postulated a so-called "general will," a common acknowledgment of those reciprocal rights and duties that can serve as the basis of the state. As the condition through which citizens would deliver their political obligations to themselves, the general will was to be understood as the rational capacity of the majority to determine the optimal social, moral, and political possibilities by which the group could realize its best interests. These interests can only be adequately determined by a will that is general in principle, and not simply an expression of a self-interested minority. Indeed, the general will by virtue of its superior authenticity and representation may force the recalcitrant individual to be "free" by the standards it imposes on him; to be "free" meant to be part of the general will and to live one's "real inner nature"—to live in conformity to the innermost social requirements.

Rousseau's sanctification of the general will came to imply that it is the final judge of the optimal social and moral possibilities of the individual. Further, through its determination of individual rights and duties, the general will may nullify any doctrine of natural rights. Individuals must surrender through the social contract those rights and liberties which it is vital for the community to control. Any sovereign power can only exist in the people as a whole, and legitimate political society will become an expression of their general will. Here we have *in ovo* the foundations of both the collective and totalitarian states of the nineteenth and twentieth centuries that would follow Rousseau. In the nineteenth century the state would come to be seen as the agent which must restore the collective equality of the previous state of nature. Also from Rousseau's influence it would come to be assumed in Kierkegaard's Denmark that human beings are essentially social creatures whose possibilities and rights are to be established by the collective and by politics. These assumptions would develop into the subsequent liberal and totalitarian politics of Europe and they would be followed by the Rousseauist assumption that the human being is good by original nature; that he or she is corrupted only through the artificialities and defects of the post-state-of-nature societies. The final consequence of these assumptions for the world that Kierkegaard would inherit was that there would be no room or awareness for a theological or Christian identification of spiritual calamities in the present age. Even in Kierkegaard's provincial Denmark there would be a positive reception of Rousseau's assumptions as they came to pervade European society. Kierkegaard came to reject most of these, and he challenged their pervasive influence in his theology and his doctrines of the mass, the individual, and salvation.

(C) Schelling

Another important, but constructive, influence upon Kierkegaard was the teachings of Friedrich Wilhelm von Schelling (1775-1854) at the University of Berlin. Schelling was the only important philosopher whom Kierkegaard actually heard when he was a student there. Hegel had died in 1831 when Kierkegaard was eighteen and still a student at the University of Copenhagen. Schelling's so-called "positive philosophy" provided a reactive agent to the Hegelianism that Kierkegaard had imbibed at the University of Copenhagen, and it helped to establish the conceptualizations that Kierkegaard would later utilize in his negative ascriptions to the crowd. Schelling drew for the young Kierkegaard the distinction between a negative and positive philosophy. By a "negative philosophy" Schelling referred to any philosophical attempt, such as that of Hegel, which would seek to identify beings solely by their conceptual properties or their cognitively identifiable "whatness." Traditionally, the medieval philosophers had understood the "whatness" of a being as essence, i.e., those characteristics without which an entity could not be defined as what it is. In scholastic thought this "whatness" was termed the *quid est* of something, the whatever-it-is that gives an entity the identity it has and not another. Schelling believed that his "positive philosophy" had its genesis in the contrary medieval thesis that the brute existence of something, its "that-ness" (*quod est*), designates a positive presence of something prior to its conceptual identity. The "that-ness" of something places emphasis upon the actual being or existence that precedes its essential nature. This "that-it-is-ness" of something was for the medieval philosophers, and later for Schelling, prior to its "what-it-is-ness." Such a priority is "positive" in the sense that an entity's actual existence is the foremost way that it has being, and the foremost way that something is encountered.

Schelling's prime philosophical enemy was Hegel, and Hegel held, according to Schelling, that essence was both prior to and of greater reality than existence. For Hegel it was only essence which could be grasped by reason. Further, the Absolute Reality could only take the form of thought. Conceptual knowability had become in Hegel the primary characteristic of the world. Schelling, on the other hand, believed that authentic philosophy must reveal the actual or positive existence of something, and not be confined to any rationalistic essentialism. For Schelling Hegel's system had in fact ignored the positive "that-it-is" perspective upon being. It had also nullified the priority of actual existence, especially that of the individual. Schelling would make individuated existence central to his thought, especially in his late *Philosophie der Mythologie* and *Philosophie der Offenbarung*. His basic formulation of the philosophical problematic was posed as the question, "Why is there something instead of nothing?" He also asked, "How do we understand the existence of individuals?" Both of these questions became central to the thought of Kierkegaard.

While the mature Kierkegaard would have little sympathy for Schelling's philosophical system as a whole, he would fully appropriate Schelling's claim that Hegel's philosophy could never adequately grasp the individuated, actual existence of beings, especially human being. He also accepted Schelling's proto-existential thesis that human existence is possessed as immediate experience, and Kierkegaard would claim with Schopenhauer, Nietzsche, Dilthey, Bergson, Heidegger, and Ortega y Gasset that the existence which is given most immediately and fully to the individual is one's own. Immediate experience reveals to individuals that their existence is more than cognitive or rational. To Kierkegaard it revealed that we are also volitional, emotive, valuating, and self-transcending beings. Kierkegaard's thought would reject both Plato and Hegel's assumption that the abstractions of conceptual being enjoy a higher status than individuated, actual existence. Further, Kierkegaard would maintain that our individual existence cannot be abstractly constituted through the Hegelian mediations of the individual into society, the economy, or the state. Such abstract entities and the negative philosophy that produces them are but preludes to the coming of mass society.

(D) Kierkegaard's Life and Work as an Existential Thinker

Among Schelling's students at the University of Berlin was the young Kierkegaard. This attentive scholar had been born in Copenhagen on May 15, 1813. As the son of a prosperous and intellectually inclined father, he had received from him a rigorous informal education in both theology and philosophy. The father suffered from depression, and the young Kierkegaard seems to have inherited this malady which he bore all of his life. He entered the University of Copenhagen in the faculty of theology, but philosophy and literature were his more vital concerns at the time. He gained at the university a knowledge of the Hegelianism which had come to dominate so many of the theological and philosophical faculties of Europe, but he later came to react against this doctrine, because it could not supply what he claimed he needed, "a truth for me," a truth for which he could "live or die." After his graduation from the university in 1840, he traveled to Germany, where he came to sit before Schelling in Berlin. Schelling maintained in his lectures that Hegel's so-called "negative philosophy" neglected and despised actual existence, especially that of the individual. While Kierkegaard ingested Schelling's "positive philosophy" with some gusto, he still regarded Hegel as the greatest of speculative philosophers. While Kierkegaard later attacked Hegel's system, he nevertheless inherited from him such philosophical elements as the dialectical stages of individual development, historicality of existence, and dialectical thought generally. Section E will develop Hegel's influence.

The young Kierkegaard became alienated from the Danish National Lutheran Church, which his father had firmly supported. A cynical observer of this state-supported national Christianity, Kierkegaard joined the hedonistic life of secular Copenhagen. Yet he soon posed to himself the question of how the individual could be raised from the disillusionment that seemed to accompany the life he had chosen. In this period he experienced a religious and emotional conversion, and he attempted to inculcate some moral standards into a life which seems to have become oriented to despair. He returned firmly to his theological studies and prepared to become a pastor in the established Danish church. Upon the death of his father he became engaged to the seventeen-year-old Regina Olsen. But he soon broke the engagement, because he came to believe that he had a mission which made him unsuited for marriage and which demanded of him a life devoted to Christian authorship. The year 1843 saw the publication of his *Either-Or, A Fragment of Life* and also his *Fear and Trembling,* books which gained him national recognition. In 1844 there appeared *The Concept of Dread* and *Philosophical Fragments,* and in 1846 *Concluding Unscientific Postscript* and subsequently the *Two Ages.* The latter is the focal work of our present study. Many of his books were published under different pseudonyms to indicate that he was writing objective and indirect communications, rather than the convictions of a converted Christian; at a later stage, however, he tended to express himself more directly as a personal advocate, in such works as *The Sickness unto Death* (1849) and *Attack upon "Christendom"* (1855). Yet in these later works he abstained from the construction of either a theological or a philosophical system. Indeed, formal systematics, especially the Hegelian philosophy, were to be his special targets of attack in his later life.

Kierkegaard lived a withdrawn life as an author, but he involved himself in two public controversies that were to have a profound effect upon his attempt to conceptualize the crowd philosophically. The first of these involved his denunciation of the policies and standards of the popular Copenhagen satirical newspaper *The Corsair.* For this attack the paper so caricatured and belittled him that it contributed to his mental depression and early death—the first philosophical martyr of the mass media. The second controversy involved his doctrinal attack upon the established Danish church. In the *Attack upon "Christendom"* (1854-55) he argued that this institution was not an authentic Christianity. The national church had become, he thought, a repository of conformity and passionless moral humanism. Its emphasis was no longer upon the original Christian message, but upon a secular and comfortable national church. While Kierkegaard perceived the contemporary church leadership as only a part of the demoralization of his time, he focused his attack upon the church's official hierarchy. This was an especially aggressive strategy, because the former primate of the church, Bishop Mynster, was a friend of Kierkegaard's father. When Professor Hans Martenson claimed that Mynster had been "a witness to the truth," Kierkegaard could no longer contain his criticism of the established church. Kierkegaard had held a suppressed contempt for what he considered to be Mynster's inauthentic Christianity. To augment the problem, Martensen became in 1854 the bishop of the Danish church. A Hegelian, Martensen believed that any critical subjectivity on the part of individuals was a "mere romanticism" which must be replaced by the Hegelian "objective reason" in the church and state. But for Kierkegaard such an attitude would result in a species of passionless conformity that would spell the death of any authentic Christianity that remained in Europe. He opened a series of attacks in which he attempted to reveal the incompatibility of the church's conformity, secularism, and bureaucracy with the inward passion of early Christian faith. Kierkegaard died shortly after this controversy in 1855 (at age 42), after he had refused on his deathbed the church's sacraments. The epitaph he wished for his grave was "That Individual." This wish, properly understood, is one key to his attack upon the Hegelian philosophy, the mass, and his critique of modernism.

It is perhaps best to approach Kierkegaard's philosophical-theological position on mass society through a brief outline of his doctrine of the self. For him the self is the bearer of subjective experiences which are constantly being assembled into a coherent whole. Here Kierkegaard accepted the doctrine of the self as it had been developed in classical German idealism since Kant and Hegel. In this tradition the human being is understood primarily as self-consciousness. For Kierkegaard self-consciousness indicates that the self can know, cognize, remember, and project itself from out of its interiority. In a famous passage Kierkegaard defined the self as follows:

A human being is a spirit. But what is a spirit? Spirit is the self. But what is the self? The self is a relation which relates itself to itself . . . A human being is a synthesis of the infinite and finite, of possibility and necessity, of the eternal and the temporal. In short, a synthesis. A synthesis is a relation between two factors. Looked at in this way, a human being is not yet a self.[1]

The self, then, consists in the fact that it relates itself to its own self. The self is also a "spirit," a self-possessed, autonomous being which can resist external controls. "Spirit" possesses the knowledge or awareness that it is a self-relation to the world. The self is autonomous and infinite in its ability to transcend its worldly circumstances through its recognition of its own possibilities. But the self is radically finite in that it must always address the immediate and contingent aspects of its world. In short, the self exists in a series of existential paradoxes. The first of these is that the self is a combination of natural restraints and non-natural possibilities. The self possesses both freedom and imagination, through which it is autonomous; yet at the same time the self must still exist in a world of pressing actualities. The self does not possess any final rules or habits by which it can confront either its own possibilities or its worldly actualities. These paradoxes suggest that the self is both a natural and a non-natural being.

As a dialectical pair of both natural and non-natural elements, the self is also the center of the will, which holds its parts together in a totality. Here the will is a "positive third term" which acts to attain the possibilities of personhood. Yet the positivity of the self's autocreation through its possibilities cannot prevent an anxiety which it can never lose and for which there is no cure. We always remain a bundle of unfulfilled possibilities, and because of their unfulfillment, we remain anxious beings. It is through the capacity for self-creation that the person can for Kierkegaard be counted a non-natural being. Because we possess the possibility to create a world different from the one we actually inhabit, we must live with possibility as a part of our person. Since human beings possess no pre-given forms for the working out of their possibilities, we are anxious before the finite and eternal, the natural and non-natural. Anxiety (*angest*) is a constant characteristic of the self, a craving for what we both desire and fear. For Kierkegaard what we dominantly desire and fear is freedom. We both desire and fear to escape from that freedom to which God has called us. Such an escape from freedom constitutes a loss of the eternal, and in the escape or forgetfulness of our freedom, our deepest spiritual ground, we come to despair. All scientific analysis of the self forgets this fact. It forgets that the self is significantly nonnatural; that the self's deepest nature is the capacity for self-determination in historical time. Natural science forgets that the self's existence can never be separated from time and becoming; that the form that time and becoming take in human life is history.

This historicality of the self was seen by Kierkegaard to have its roots both in the Judeo-Christian biblical tradition and in Hegel, and this historicality was later understood from Dilthey to Heidegger and Ortega y Gasset as *Lebenszeit* (lived time). Kierkegaard recognized that there is a distinction between the external motion of nature and the historical temporality of the self. The self's historicality is not grounded in natural law, or in any logical necessity. Because the self reveals no such logical or lawlike necessity, human life must be understood non-naturalistically as the historicity of choice, possibility, and contingency in our temporal existence. It was one of Kierkegaard's great insights to have discovered that the individual "becomes" in a unique manner. The self cannot be, indeed will not be, understood as a mere succession of physical things or events. The self is an autofabrication which we may affirm or repress as the task of becoming. We "become" in the natural world *and*, for Kierkegaard, we become as participants in the eternal, which is our final ground.

Part of Kierkegaard's task as an author was to ask how our individual subjective existence is possible in the present age. This question is central both to Kierkegaard and to the theme of this study, for his life's work was in great part the attempt to counteract the dissolution of the individual in this so-called age of the individual. For Kierkegaard the issue of the individual is usually raised in the context of the question of how we may become Christians. And this question is the residue of his construction of the stages on life's way, the conditions through which the person must pass to become fully individuated before the eternal. These stages are usually listed as the aesthetic, ethical, and religious. Yet for Kierkegaard there is still another stage, "the public," which is the chief concern of this study. But before we can understand this term, it is necessary to designate the context of stages in which this fourth term appears.

The aesthetic stage is one of feeling and self-expansion; it is often typified by Kierkegaard in the young, though it must not be restricted to this class. Here the individual's life is dominated by sensation, impulse, and pleasure. The individual's existence takes the form of self-dispersion and experiment without definite moral standards. The individual lives as a "spectator" whose primary goal is to maximize sensation and to avoid the personal involvements of work, marriage, or definite orientation. This individual may be the aspiring artist or youthful academic who seeks to represent his or her existence through a limitless range of artistic or scholastic experiences. This individual may seek to establish dominance and importance through experimental life styles. Attempting to realize as many possibilities and sensations as he can, the individual may come to realize that the attainment of various postures will leave only temporary satisfactions. Such satisfactions will so often result in pain and boredom that the individual slides into discontent or despair.

In such a status of disenchantment the individual will often direct his or her possibilities to the stage of the ethical. The ethical is the stage of such universals as career, marriage, or society. In the ethical demands of family and career, both self-actualization and ethical universality are assumed to be realized. The individual seems convinced that an authentic moral existence has replaced the previous aesthetic stage of feeling and self-gratification. The fullness of human life appears to have been attained in the secular universal of the ethical. Life seems to the individual to have exhausted all possibilities in its attainment. But the individual is often threatened by the suspicion that the universality of the ethical is not certain. Nor does it seem final that our will and choices have fulfilled whatever moral prescriptions we have been assuming. Secular-universal orientation comes to seem, as in the case of the aesthetic stage, to be incomplete and of dubious import or meaning. At this stage, if not earlier, the individual may come to an awareness of the tragic dimensions of finitude, sin, guilt, and death. Our former projections of the stages of life as sensation and duty have become tenuous and dissatisfying. Our final individual need, the eternal, has not been addressed or even adequately formulated as a possibility of the individual's life.

For Kierkegaard such an unresolved condition, a condition of human life itself, can only be addressed by what he calls a passionate choice, "a leap of faith." Such a "leap" is the person's final attempt to appropriate a truth or status that makes complete our unfulfilled individuality or self-actualization. Seeking a passionate and inward commitment, the individual has come to realize in this third stage that the truth of our individual subjectivity is not to be had by sensate experiences, by ethical deeds or postures, by social participation or scholarship or reason. The plight of our individual existence can only be finally addressed by a commitment to the eternal. Here our uncertainty before final things is not totally resolved, for our "leap" is itself into a dimension which is unfathomed from the individual's perspective. But our orientation to the eternal, appropriated through faith, is held to be the only possible resolution for the ambiguities and unresolvedness of our ultimate concern. The individual has to come to believe that the final *telos* or end-goal of human life cannot be realized in sensation, ethics, or the crowd's sociality, for these end in demoralization and aborted possibility. This is the case even though the eternal can only be approached in faith, and in fear and trembling. But since Kierkegaard believed that "spirit" is the most authentic nature of personhood, it is only in the spirit's affinity for the eternal that we can ground the ultimate possibility of our life.

But it is important to note here that at any stage of personal growth the individual may fall out of one of the above-mentioned stages and fall into the "public." This is the fourth possibility, which always hovers around the other stages. It is a "stage" on life's way but also one in which the individual may become permanently fixed. Unable to generate the passion or inwardness to fix or decide an either-or (*Aut-aut*) determination regarding a definite orientation to his or her existence, the massified individual will release into a conformity and anonymity that manages to exist in union with other stages. The individual, for example, may be fully locked into the aesthetic stage, yet may still internalize the leveling process and identify with the possibilities of the crowd.

In this situation of leveling or relinquishing one's identity to that of the mass, there may occur to the individual the "despair of finitude." This despair will occur, because the usual secular attempts to address our finitude will tend to fail in historical time. The individual who realizes his despair has come to face a void in personal existence which the crowd cannot satisfy. But the crowd can make us deceive ourselves about our finitude and final goal; the crowd can expedite the individual's natural avoidance of the eternal truth of self-determination in historical time. Kierkegaard, provoked by the Hegelian assumptions that the educational, political, and religious systems of Denmark could save the individual from nihilism, fully realized the power of the crowd to make us avoid the eternal truth. It is to Kierkegaard's relation to this pervasive Hegelianism that we must now turn.

(E) Hegelianism and the Philosophical Genesis of the Crowd

It is from Rousseau and Hegel that we inherit the notion that human beings are essentially social creatures whose deepest nature is to be found in their relation to others. The thought of Kierkegaard, Nietzsche, Heidegger, and Ortega y Gasset is in significant part a protest against this thesis. They found in it both leveling and dehumanizing tendencies for the life of the individual, and for them neither our ideal nature nor our salvation is to be situated in the group. But it was Kierkegaard who first responded critically to Hegel's formulation of human sociality and its implications for the individual, and it is this issue we must now examine. Georg Wilhelm Friedrich Hegel (1770-1831) had held at the time of Kierkegaard's birth an unrivaled position at the University of Berlin. He was seen as a sort of philosophical monarch of Europe. He had been introduced to Danish intellectual life by J.L. Heiberg, the light and head of

the Royal Theatre in Copenhagen. Philosophical and theological status was also given to Hegel's teachings by the Danish
Bishop Hans Lassen Martensen. Kierkegaard could not then
have avoided Hegel's influence, as a young man who belonged
to both church and university. From an early stage in his thinking Kierkegaard had attempted to understand the theoretical
foundations of contemporary European, especially Danish,
society. Kierkegaard came to realize, slowly at first, but then
with a sort of stunned awareness, that Hegelianism was inimical
to authentic Christianity. Kierkegaard realized that Hegel—
along with the Danish National Church—was maintaining that if
individuals were left to their own autonomy and conscience,
the result could only be social and religious anarchy; intellectual
content and collective identity must be given to the individual
only through tradition, social usage, and finally identification
with the state. Hegel had maintained that romantic individualism must be replaced by the individual's acceptance of social
and political duties.[2] His thought seemed to demonstrate to
emerging modern states like Denmark that the culmination of
human development is to be found in the individual's association with the state. In this final political phase individuals would
find their most complete identity and freedom through their
association with the national group. In such a Hegelian thesis
Kierkegaard found the grounds for an attack on a philosopher
whom he had otherwise admired in certain respects.

But Kierkegaard also found other grounds for his distrust of
Hegel, in Hegel's contention that speculative philosophy is the
instrument through which knowledge of the Absolute can be
attained. Man's comprehension of the Absolute, Hegel argued,
is gained through a rational, dialectical process. Here a concept
generates its own opposite, and the resultant form becomes a
synthesis, which also acts as a new thesis. This process Hegel
identified as Becoming. Becoming, however, is more than a
logical category. It is also the historical process through which
the Absolute reveals itself. History becomes the concrete and
phenomenal manifestation of the Absolute. For Hegel it is the
office of philosophy to seek the construction of the Absolute
through the integration of all stages of consciousness, including
art, religion, and philosophy. Through the construction of the

Absolute Hegel believed he had integrated such dualisms as those that obtain between phenomena and noumena, and the individual and society.

In his *Spirit of Christianity* (1798-1799) the young Hegel had maintained that our finite existence participated in the infinite through Christ. Divine love (*agape*) was the means of mediation between our finite existence and the infinite. The essence of humanity was spirit (*Geist*), through which we achieved union with God. But by the time of the Phenomenology of Spirit (1807) Hegel came to hold that only the methods of philosophical idealism could express in systematic form the relation of both the finite and infinite to the Absolute. Here the Absolute came for him to be the philosophical expression of the idea of divinity in the older Christian tradition. The belief of the young Hegel that the Christian religion was the embodiment of the Absolute was rejected. Further, it became the end of philosophy to think the Absolute in conceptual and not intuitive terms. Philosophical knowledge was the awareness that the mind has of itself. Intelligibility was only attained through the identity of thought and its object. The Absolute devolved from the transcendent God of Christianity to the thought that thinks itself. Everything then depended upon the capacity of thought to think itself as subject as well as object. Here the subject came to know itself through the stages of art, religion, and philosophy as conceptual moments in the attainment of absolute self-consciousness. Further, Hegel understood the religious stage of consciousness as a lower one than philosophy, which conceived the Absolute. This was the case, he believed, because religion stated only by means of feeling, sense images, symbols, and theological authority what philosophy was able to state conceptually and systematically.

Before he heard Schelling at the University of Berlin, Kierkegaard had believed that the philosophical task of his era was to translate as much of Hegel's stages of consciousness as possible into the terms of personal existence. These emerged in Kierkegaard's work as the stages on life's way and the dialectical and historical usages that permeated his thought. Kierkegaard posed for himself this goal in his writing in spite of the fact that he was generally disillusioned with philosophy. When professional philosophers seek to proclaim the nature of the real, it is as misleading as seeing a sign being sold in a store which announces "Pressing is done here"; the sign is in fact only intended to be sold by the store, so that if we bring our clothes to such a place, we shall have been deceived. In like manner Kierkegaard believed that Hegel's system was misleading if we believed that it could address itself to the demands of the individual's actual existence.

Further, in his *Concluding Unscientific Postscript* (1846) Kierkegaard argued that traditional philosophy in general, and Hegelianism in particular, avoided the priority of human existence as the mode of being which is immediately and primordially experienced by the individual. The *Postscript* can be significantly understood as an attack upon Hegel's tendency to replace the primacy of this existence with that of thought.[3] For Kierkegaard existence, and especially human existence (*Existenz*), is the state of being actually and objectively there. Human existence is individual being that is considered to be reality, as it is given to the person. Human existence is from the beginning undemonstrated and always assumed. In their thinking and action human beings always reason from and never towards existence. This implies that existence is never a philosophical or theoretical derivation, but always that from which thought and action proceed. Kierkegaard believed that Hegel had substituted for the actuality and immediacy of this existence the essentiality of reason, especially in his systematic construction of the real. This rationalism revealed itself most totally in Hegel's doctrine of essence (*Wesen*). Essence for him was the intelligible aspect of existence, and as such it was the first category and primary possibility of being. Primary being for Hegel was conceptual being, which could be considered independently of its primary there-ness. The identity of a thing or event thus became its conceptual nature in abstraction from its primacy as actual existence.

However, for Kierkegaard the abstract universality of thought or of essence cannot constitute adequate reality or primary being. Existence must always be confined to a particular individual. Any merely conceptual or essential is-ness that we ascribe to the particular individual cannot be its actuality, but only its abstract form. Primary being, on the other hand, is that which is an actuality in space, time, or human life. If this primary being were restricted to only the logical or the essentially conceivable, then this real being would be identical to the conceptual categories of the Hegelian Absolute. For Kierkegaard the Hegelian distinction between actual and conceptual implied that essence was a category prior to existence. While Kierkegaard recognized essence as a logical category, he held as a proto-existentialist that primary reality is existence, the brute actuality of something. Essence always arises from a prior existence. In this sense human existence is always prior to any objective or conceptual abstractions, and Hegel abandoned existence for his logical and conceptual understanding of the real. Such essentialism must be replaced by the existential thinking of primary existence. Only this can address the concrete ethical, religious, and social demands that confront the individual. Such demands require the subjective commitment of the individual's life, and not the conceptualizations of the abstract thinker.

In sum, for Kierkegaard the Hegelian system could never see that thought and being are not co-extensive; that the actuality of human existence is not merely conceptual. Hegel's fundamental term, the concept (*Begriff*), is not for Kierkegaard identical to the real. Such an identity could only be achieved by the conceptual repression of the existing individual. The individual's existence, then, is always prior to any thematized conceptualization of it. But because the "abstract philosopher" has conflated thought and existence, the indication is that he does not know what it actually means to exist. At best, he declines the individual into a merely observational and theoretical entity. And this is the inevitable result of the Hegelian conception of truth as the conformity of thought and being, the identity of the real and the rational. The general argument of the *Postscript* is that whenever thought and being are equated in truth, the result will be the nullification of the individual.

The Hegelian and Kierkegaardian doctrines of truth are at the heart of this situation, and the divergence between Hegelian essentialism and Kierkegaardian existentialism is nowhere more prominent than in Kierkegaard's doctrine of truth as inwardness or subjectivity. It was primarily in his *Postscript* that he formulated his position on this issue. His doctrine here represents the Danish thinker's attempt to formulate a philosophical alternative to the objective, especially Hegelian, formulations of truth that had come to dominate contemporary Europe. It should be noted at once that Kierkegaard's doctrine is not the traditional ascription of truth to the relation of thought to object in a one-to-one correspondence between the terms of a proposition and the elements of some objective fact. Such a thesis would represent truth as an *adequatio* of thought to objective being. But Kierkegaard's notion of truth does not refer to the adequation of concept and object, or to the knowledge of the universally valid propositions of science, or to Hegel's Absolute. Truth is a characteristic of the individual's inwardness with respect to the ultimate concern which is primarily an object of faith and uncertainty. Truth is that passionate inwardness to which we voluntarily commit ourselves through the appropriation of the objectively uncertain.[4] Such a commitment requires for Kierkegaard a "leap of faith" that is often "an offense to reason." In this sense, Kierkegaard's doctrine of subjective truth refers to that inwardness which transforms our existence through choice and faith.

The individual is assumed in this doctrine to possess an existence whose implications extend beyond theoretical awareness to the areas of will, freedom, and the ultimate concerns of faith. But he believed modern man has forgotten what such inwardness can mean. Contemporary, secular man, he believed, tends to understand truth exclusively as a property of natural science. But our self-actualization in faith is not aided by such a truth. Hegel had attempted to reveal the nature of truth by tracing the history of consciousness, whose phases are in dialectical opposition. But for Kierkegaard this rationalism had produced a "dialectical masked man" who had seemingly escaped the domain of subjective truth and commitment-through-faith. Hegel's individual remained a philosophical construction whose rational activity achieved only a theoretical identification with the Absolute.

Kierkegaard once remarked, as we noted before, that if he should ever have an inscription for his tombstone, he would desire none other than "That Individual." In part, this wish referred to the fact that his life's mission was to reinstate the individual before God. This reinstatement was a project for his personal existence; it was also the philosophical project of the appropriation of the individual to the Christian *telos*. Kierkegaard saw that Hegel's individual was only a theoretical creation whose ultimate end was unification of the "I" with the thinking of the Absolute. Both of these ends fell short of an authentic spiritual *telos* for the concrete individual. Kierkegaard's own conception of the individual is a complex one that will unfold in many sections of chapters ahead. At this point we can only skim the surface to say that for him the human being is a synthesis of the finite and eternal, whose absolute *telos* is the eternal; yet the synthesis is of an uneasy nature; the individual in his or her inward subjectivity remains aware both of a separation from the eternal and of a dependency upon it for final happiness. The individual feels a call from each direction, from the finite and the eternal; he or she is tempted on the one hand to seek finite, secular substitutes for the eternal, because of the need to escape despair; but he or she is also continually responsible to the call of the eternal. Only the eternal *telos*, though it is hoped for in fear and trembling, can finally release us from despair. The re-turning of the individual to this source or goal can only be accomplished through a leap of faith. This being so, salvation implicitly excludes political, economic, or humanistic means to this end. The socio-economic aggregate (the group or crowd or mass) cannot be so "edified" or raised up to the eternal, because the mass is untruth, and the individual captured within it denies man's authentic *telos* to the divine. Kierkegaard pointed out that Christ, even while addressing the multitude, spoke essentially to each individual. Modern Christianity often fails to understand that the greatest contemporary danger to its survival is the declension of the individual into the mass. If the individual is to be a Christian, he or she must attempt to resist absorption into it; and only by reference to a transcendent point can the individual avoid the modern tendency to deify the mass. This transcendent point was not provided by Hegel, because Kierkegaard saw his thought and that of the present age as a deification of the "we." Merold Westpahl has argued that spirit, for Hegel and for mass society, has devolved into the unity of self-consciousness in society, "an I that has become a we, and a we that is I." "I am who we are," and the "we" cannot be separated from the I's who make it up.[5] In short, for Kierkegaard Hegel's thought is the theoretical triumph of the mass in the present age. We must now examine this mass more closely.

Chapter Two

The Phantom Public

(A) The Danish Background

Kierkegaard saw the rise of the masses against the background of the liberal European revolutions of 1848. While these revolutions were suspect to him, he was opposed neither to modernity per se, nor to Danish liberalism in particular. But the revolutions of 1848 were for him the beginning of a general unrest, the loss of the Danish provinces of Schleswig and Holstein to Germany, and the transformation of the Danish monarchy into a constitutional one. This was the beginning of the growth of secular egalitarianism in Denmark. For Kierkegaard the entire present age in Europe could only be understood in light of the political, social and economic developments after 1848. He believed that in the present age, the "age of disintegration," the masses would attempt to reduce all existential and moral problems to political and social ones. For Danish leadership everything would become a matter of manipulating the crowd to their point of view. Given such a situation, Kierkegaard believed that it would be impossible to count on any mass support for a Danish Christian monarch who derived authority from God; Denmark would be transformed into a limited constitutional monarchy. The new political establishment would demand that both royal and individual powers be limited.

Royalism was a prominent element in Kierkegaard's political beliefs from about 1830 to 1839, but after the revolutions of 1848 he moved away from this position, and he considered political radicalism of left or right to be harmful to the attainment of the person's individuation. His *Two Ages*, though written two years before 1848, is often understood as a counteraction to radicalism. But here Kierkegaard's efforts are to be contrasted to those of someone like J.L. Heiberg, who wanted to counteract radicalism through the imposition of Hegelianism on the Danish polity, as an attempt to provide unity to the state. From the beginning Kierkegaard rejected any attempt to revise or stabilize Danish national life through the importation of foreign philosophies. But in spite of his opposition to Heiberg, Kierkegaard can be classed as a member of the Danish conservative tradition. Kierkegaard supported the Lutheran doctrine of "call and station," and he was never opposed to the social, economic, and educational stratification of Danish society. Further, he also held that Denmark must remain a Christian state, even though medieval society was nominally exhausted. The Danish Christian state could be "liberal" to the extent that it would address social and personal problems through charity; but it should never attempt to level socio-economic classes or to redistribute income. For Kierkegaard the state—Danish or other —is an example of human egotism "written large." When the state assumes the posture of promoting mass egalitarianism, he believed, it has become Satan "disguised as an angel of light." Kierkegaard devoted his political thought to the refutation of the Platonic doctrine that the state must be "written large" in order to grasp more adequately the nature of political virtues. Kierkegaard attempted to deconstruct the entire Platonic approach to politics. He felt that the modern search for political virtue and equality since the Enlightenment had enabled Europe to overcome some social and political tyrannies, but the tyranny of the crowd had arisen to take their place. Kierkegaard recognized in this respect that after the French Revolution the crowd would be increasingly appealed to as the means of all political reform in Europe. He also saw that the conflicts that have come to dominate the present age are political ones. It is the illusion of the present age that final purposes can be instrumented through politics. But the actual condition of the present age prohibits this assumption. The condition of the individual requires a more radical solution. Kierkegaard would attempt to direct his message to the individual person who is lost in the mass. It would be a message of hope for Denmark, and for mankind at large. The political and social thought which expresses this message is best contained in his *Two Ages*.

(B) *Two Ages*

Kierkegaard's reflections upon the crowd are found primarily in a long review of a now forgotten novel, *Two Ages* (1845), by a Mrs. Christine Gyllembourg (1773-1856). It is in Part III of his work, "Conclusions from a Consideration of the Two Ages," that his relevant philosophical analysis of the crowd is found. Kierkegaard's review was his first publication after the *Postscript*, and it was fully entitled *Two Ages: The Age of Revolution and the Present Age* (1846). An independent essay in its own right, the *Two Ages* was basically the occasion through which Kierkegaard could express his critique of the age in which he lived and provide a prognosis of its future. The work must also be understood as a moral, cultural, and political analysis of his own time and, by implication, our own. Kierkegaard's *Two Ages* opposed two different eras, the passionate age of revolution, especially the French Revolution, and the present age of reflection, rationalism, and the "crowd." While both ages are actually stages of modernity, which began after the overthrow of the ancient regime in France, Kierkegaard contrasted the two ages with each other as representations of modernism, as Mrs. Gyllembourg had done earlier. In his review Kierkegaard commended her novel, and he saw in her treatment of its characters the main features of the revolutionary age of France and the present age in Denmark and Europe. Through his review of the novel, then, Kierkegaard managed to produce a critique of the whole of modernity, which he designated as "the present age."

In his *Two Ages* Kierkegaard developed a brief philosophy of history which outlined the basic periods of the West.[1] The first stage he designated "the dialectic of antiquity." There the masses were subordinated to a superior, such as a caesar, who enjoyed absolute power yet who was able to grant social and moral significance to the individuals below him. This period was followed by the so-called "dialectic of Christendom," in which individuals attempted to free themselves from despotism, and to install those rulers who would be restrained by the final authority of God. This stage characterized the medieval period, and was followed by the "age of revolution," typified by the French Revolution. This age was one of passion, loyalty, will, and imagination. Devoted to revolution and justice, the age of passion attempted to relate individuals to those ideals that their era strove to attain. Persons could achieve their worth and identity through individual commitment, personal loyalties, and revolutionary enthusiasms. The "passion" of this age was due, Kierkegaard believed, to the fact that this age had not suspended the principle of existential contradiction. There the individual or the group attempted to decide and act upon either good or evil, to be devoted or not devoted to something. Such distinctions remained essential in the age of revolution. But in the late eighteenth and early nineteenth centuries there began to appear what Mrs. Gyllembourg and Kierkegaard called "the present age." This age is typified by a blurred distinction between such contradictions as good and evil, equal and unequal, passionate and reflective. It is an age of "sensible reflection" and "passionless projects" which flare up and then relax into indolence. It is an age of reflection and abstraction which forgets the former age's emphasis upon action and decision, for these have been replaced by the spectations and observations of a passive public. Individuals relate to each other not through loyalty, but through such abstractions as "democracy" or "freedom." Afraid of boredom, the present age must be presented with spectacles, such as politics, sports, sensational trials, entertainment, and group performances. The present age is a spectatorial society.[2] In this stage the concrete individual tends to be nullified as an ethical and responsible entity, and the category of the "public" arises. We shall examine this category subsequently in some detail. The final stage of Kierkegaard's philosophy of history is simply "the future," a stage that will arise when the mass public has destroyed all social cohesion and individual identity. Here, when individuals realize that they have become lost in the public, and can find no resolution for their state in the secular mass, they may turn to the individuality of their final *telos* in the infinite. At this point individuals will have tired themselves with vanity, and they may attempt to "leap over the blade" of their leveled existence into the religious stage. In the light of this general philosophy of history, we must examine our present age in greater detail, and ask how it got to be as it is.

In his *Two Ages* Kierkegaard's basic plan was to distinguish between the prior ages and the modern era. By the "modern era" Kierkegaard intended primarily his own century, in which he saw the leveling tendency and the rule of the crowd as the predominant form of social life. The chief features of the present age, as we saw, are the loss of passion and the loss of commitment. The age of heroic action is over, and great deeds are anticipated only for coming generations. Because heroic conditions are only anticipated, heroic action is not expected in the present. Any recognition of an actual hero or leader seems based on envy, not admiration. Heroic motives are assigned to everyone and no one; leadership seems to belong to everyone and no one; leaders seem to lack authority; and even political passion seems to be exhausted.

Passion plays a central role in Kierkegaard's understanding of human development. In the *Two Ages*, we recall, it is the absence of passion that becomes the paramount feature of modernity. Yet if there is one authentic passion still possessed by the modern age, it is envy. Envy (*misundelse*) is the emotion which seems to give identity to the contemporary individual. Though characterized by faltering enthusiasms and evasive commitments, the individual in the present age possesses only the "negatively unifying principle" of envy. This envy was related by Kierkegaard to the "thralldom of reflection."[3] Just as enthusiasm and passion were the unifying principles of the age of revolution, so envy is the unifying principle of the modern age. Kierkegaard understood envy to be a resentment against those who through their spirit or status assume themselves to be "above" others. It is the power of envy which is able in the modern age to unify the mass against those who assume such a status. Here envy becomes related to a desire for power, and not to the desire for justice or helpfulness; envy is not actively for something, and it often joins forces with indolence and cowardice.

But envy refuses to remain in the abstract form we have given it so far. It insists upon taking a concrete form, oriented to the claim to superiority that is most easily comprehended by other individuals—the possession of money. Money is that possession which in the modern age is universally envied. What we own and what we are able to buy are for Kierkegaard the major criteria that provide significant identity to the individuals of the present age. The concrete relations of family, friendship, and profession are neglected, and the individual becomes identified with his or her place in the economic nexus of society. Here our most significant decisions and commitments are dissolved into economic calculations. Because money is the final *telos* to which we are expected to devote our lives, a monetary superiority over others becomes the major passion of the crowd. In the age of reflection this passion reveals our tendency to barbarism and decadence. Indeed, envy reveals itself in the individual as jealousy, resentment, and fear.

Another way in which envy exhibits itself is the egotism through which the individual assumes an intellectual superiority over others. This form of self-regard is notorious, said Kierkegaard, for lacking an understanding of its power or limits or effect upon others. Self-appraisal becomes joined to the abstract, quiet envy of the age of reflection. Here the individual is absorbed into the "thralldom of reflection," a state of abstraction created by the mass for the serious attention and allegiance of the individual. In the state of intellectual envy the individual supposes himself "raised up" to moral or social significance by the possession of abstract ideas; but the individual's devotion to these ideas is the opposite of the passionate situation of the revolutionary age. There individuals were raised up and others overthrown, openly, according to their loyalties and associations; in the age of reflection, on the other hand, individuals are assumed equally associated by reference to shared abstractions. This sociality rejects any individual responsibility or goals apart from group ideas. It is at this point that a "pure humanity" appears as a higher negativity in which the individual is dissolved. This "thralldom of reflection" instantly disregards or nullifies any individual orientation to a final *telos*, especially the end-goal of faith or the eternal.

These tendencies are grounded in what Robert Perkins has termed "ethical envy."[4] This is an envy which demands that all life styles be considered of equal value and significance. It constructs a republic of abstract equals, a "phantom public" which is created from a process of abstract leveling. In this way ethical envy emerges as a public phenomenon. The phenomenon of abstract leveling has created a "phantom," a public which is a "monstrous nonentity," a something that is nothing, which is generated by the age of reflection. In order to reduce everyone to the same level, the public must advance the aims of the egalitarian order by abstracting away all concrete relations. This abstract nonentity, the public, is not composed of real persons; it is everyone and nobody, an aggregate of units who have no names. As a class of abstract spectators, it can create nothing real or helpful. Leveling has become an "abstract victory over the individual." Ethical envy has here achieved a sort of equality, but only in the inauthentic sense of an individual's likeness to others. Concrete communal relations are lost, and we achieve humanity only as equals, never as individuals or inwardly significant others. The individual who was previously responsible to eternity has been replaced by an equality of numbers, and the individual has been relegated to the crowd. Here the crowd becomes a negative, abstract humanity, and no secular force can save the individual from this negativity.[5]

The mass, then, has become the abstract sociology of the present age. Possessed with only the passion for money, the present age is given over to this dominant envy, and the enthusiasms of the revolutionary age are exhausted. With the fading of ideals and of the individual's passion for the infinite, the world tends to become meaningless for the individual. The "coiled springs" of human life tend to lose force. Lacking the passions for character and inwardness, the individual is abandoned to self-orientation without a craving for ethical or religious status. Our need for others remains external and without depth, and we drift into idle talk and social spectation.

The politics of the present age will be dominated by the crowd. Politics will be joined to urbanization and to the media, and the individual will become increasingly confined to the aesthetic stage of existence. "Democracy" will be the name the crowd gives to "the gigantic something" of egalitarian society. A mere numerical abstraction, the crowd will pose as a final moral reality. Mass democracy will allow to society only economics as the last concrete relation. Leveling will dim down all other forms of social interaction to the most abstract or rudimentary levels.

Kierkegaard assumed that the masses have always existed, even in the ancient world. But Kierkegaard was the first to see that in the present age the crowd is of a unique nature. The crowd is beyond the traditional mass of the past, for it exists as a phantom of qualitative uniformity, an abstraction which is a permanent possibility of ourselves. Yet it is continually unrepentant and self-satisfied. It is true that the tendency of the unrepentant public in the past was toward a type of leveling through revolution and upheavals. But these historical phenomena were not leveling in the sense of the present age, for they were generated out of particular socio-economic interests and concrete relations. The phantom public as Kierkegaard conceived it was not forthcoming in the past, because social aggregates behaved as particular historical peoples, generations, or representatives of distinct classes and interests. Individuals remained relatively concrete, in spite of their allegiance to groups. Reflection had not created the phantom of public man in whom individuals are supposed to participate and to find their highest possibilities. There was no public stage in which the individual was supposed to find an abstract participation. In the present "age of reflection" the individual no longer relates as a subject to a sovereign state, but as a unit who is a pale image of a phantom. Here all relations become external and objective, and individuals become spectators of themselves as mere abstractions and reflections of the mass. Individual inwardness is lost in the "tension of reflection." The term "reflection" itself takes on a different meaning in the "age of reflection." It no longer refers to active, personal thinking or cognitions; it refers instead to our role as spectators, and to our de-personalized speculations about the mass events external to us; everything tends to become a spectator sport for us—we watch or "reflect" on the spectacles of life around us, be they athletic or political, judicial or religious; we take them all as news events that we can look at "objectively" and abstractly and, above all, passively and impersonally. This passive relationship is not to the eternal or even to a concrete person, but to the collective abstractions which are the chief features of the present age. The abstractions of this phantom public represent for Kierkegaard the victory of leveling over the individual in the present age.[6]

In sum, it is in the thought of Kierkegaard that we first find the expression of the contemporary mass as a philosophical concept. This concept became a prominent feature of the subsequent existential philosophy that he inaugurated. It was the goal of Kierkegaard's thinking on the crowd not to save his age or the world, but to attempt to express to contemporary individuals that they are foundering. This gesture was accomplished through exposing the nature of the phantom public, in contraposition to the authentic duty of the Christian individual.[7] This public leveling is the counterfeit of the Christian life, and it has separated individuals from both authentic communal life and their eternal *telos*. While the individuals of the present age are lost in the mass, there is still hope that they may be saved in the essentiality of the religious life. Kierkegaard strove to effect this goal in the face of the fact that the average Christian still does not understand that the crowd is dangerous. Kierkegaard believed to the end that while the public does not seek self-edification, individual people may still find salvation if they can only first be led into the status of authentic individuality.

(C) "The Crowd is Untruth"

In his early writings, Kierkegaard concentrated upon the individual's relation to Christianity, and in an important sense this concern with the individual was present until his death. But by the time of his *The Point of View for My Work as an Author* (1851) and even as early as *Two Ages* (1846), there developed in his work a parallel emphasis upon the crowd or the public. Kierkegaard here came to claim that an important possibility of the individual is the crowd, and the crowd is untruth in its very nature. For Kierkegaard this crowd is not a specific group, i.e., rich or poor, secular or religious, humble or great, but an abstract possibility of all contemporary individuals. The crowd is the permanent possibility in all individuals of losing concern for their personal status and worth, and assigning themselves to something outside of themselves in an abstract "other."

The crowd is born, for Kierkegaard, when individuals assign their identity to numbers, and find an inner support for their existence in a numerical status. A numerical mass stands here in a relation of "dialectical interaction" to the individual. The individual and mass reflect each other as microcosm to macrocosm; and the individual reflects the mass by the suppression of his or her separate inwardness. The result of this situation Kierkegaard called an "idolized positive principle of sociality." Society is an "idol" in the sense that it can level the individual away from both inwardness and God, and at the same time act as an abstract power which holds the individual in a sort of positive bondage.[8] In fact, worse than amoral, the demands of mass society are "demonic," because they require that the individual surrender to them. Such surrender takes the form of believing what "they" believe, or feeling what "one" feels, or acting as "it" acts. In other words, we may come to think, feel, or act as merely one of our possibilities, as the "one" (*das Man*) of an impersonal or abstract collectivity, rather than as ourselves. Of course the individual may become aware of being outside of him or herself, and may form personal ideas and values upon which to act. These may be quite opposed to the way the "they" or "one" usually thinks and behaves. In this sense the person may become more individuated than before, and become more self-responsible and less untrue to what he or she thinks and feels. On the other hand, the crowd is that which reduces self-responsibility to a "fraction."

There are many ways in which the crowd is "untruth." First, the crowd pretends to take on individual characteristics. It does this through the appropriation of the individual into the interpersonal public "chatter" which obscures the difference between public and private, social and individual. Such chatter is not authentically personal; responsibility is lost when we pass on gossip or make "small talk" in a crowd. We may seem to express private thoughts or reveal our inner selves, but those thoughts and selves have become public. This nullification of differences (the blurring of public and private) is a form of untruth. A second way the crowd is untruth is by leaving the individual to the forces of self-dispersal and abstraction. The crowd lacks decisiveness, yet it is continually present as an abstract power of judgment over the individual. The individual becomes untrue to him or herself by dispersing personal decisions, joining the mentality of the crowd, and thereby being irresponsible and impenitent in the presence of this abstract power. Thirdly, the crowd is untruth because of its proclivity to self-deification. While it is true for Kierkegaard that the individual must be in a secret or open despair before he or she consents to the deification of the crowd, this deification remains a permanent possibility of untruth for the massified individual. For the individual in despair the crowd creates of itself a sort of idolatry in secular dress.

It was in his *Two Ages* that Kierkegaard anticipated the phenomenon that was later made famous by Turgenev, Dostoevsky, and Nietzsche—nihilism. Kierkegaard's term for this phenomenon was leveling, and by this usage he referred to the person's despair over the attainment of individuality, the loss of passion and inwardness, and the devaluation of the human personality through abstract equality. All of these factors devolve the individual into the neutral and criterion-less station of the crowd. The key feature of this leveling is the establishment of a crowd of "equals" where nobody is of a higher or lower station than another. Such an abstract equality of persons and values is the nihilism of the modern age. But the nihilism of abstract equality can, for Kierkegaard, never become a real political possibility. Human beings, save in their existence before God, are inherently unequal. The equality of the mass is but another attempt of the crowd to substitute man for God in a new religiosity. The result of such a substitution is a confusion which obscures the fact that our contemporary condition is a consequence of abandoning the eternal and seeking salvation through social or political means.

One of the political means through which leveling is achieved is the state. For Kierkegaard the state is a sort of human egotism writ large. Kierkegaard saw the state as did St. Augustine as a necessary evil, related to human egotism. For both thinkers the state is a consequence of the fall of man. As a necessary but negative entity, it possesses little positive moral significance. Its final end is usefulness rather than goodness, and this suggests that its proper role is merely practical, i.e. the preservation of law, order, and stable community practices. The state is those workable arrangements of the public order that attempt to repress human willfulness, depravity, and egotism. The state's most positive role, then, is the provision of negative sanctions and arrangements for public peace and order.

Kierkegaard's pragmatic formulation of the role of the state was an implicit rejection of Rousseau's doctrine that the state possesses the positive function of promoting the general will. For Rousseau the proper role of the masses is their utilization by the national state, and this norm was rejected from the outset by Kierkegaard. Kierkegaard also rejected the liberal assumptions of the 1848 revolutions that human reformation results from the state's legal and social arrangements for the people. Kierkegaard was not ignorant of the social and economic problems of his day, and he was never simply the friend of wealth or prosperity. He certainly never assumed the myth that it was possible to return to a golden age or an idealized state of nature. In general, he supported the revolutions of 1848, and he accepted the constitutional monarchy which followed them in Denmark. While he was generally favorable to constitutional measures of reform and even to capitalist economics, he felt that such modernist themes were ineffectual for the "reformation" of a crowd that is rooted in pride, self-deception, and envy. Yet it remains a tendency of the crowd and the state to believe with Rousseau that the problems of modernism are ultimately political ones, and the state is assumed by many to be the proper agent for the resolution of most of humanity's problems.

The crowd, then, is one of the chief features of modernism, and Kierkegaard's thought is the attempt to confront it and minimize its authority. As one of the catastrophes that confronts the present age, the crowd emerges from a Western civilization that has lost its Christian foundation. A secular surrogate for this foundation has arisen; it is the idea of progress, through which the crowd takes upon itself the possibility of secular salvation. Salvation is assumed to result from any secular surrogate put forth by modern utopian politics, liberal, socialist, or otherwise. The mass assumption of secular perfectionism that flourished in the nineteenth century also tended to assume the state as the chief agent to this end. The new secular absolute of the mass became the state, especially as it assumed the form of Hegel's objective reason. The state, therefore, was more than a political organization based on common territory under a nominal government. The recently imported Hegelianism in Denmark carried the following assumptions. Contemporary human activity leads to the institutions of private property and public law. The individual's dialectical relation to these institutions results in a synthesis which is called the ethical order, which eventuates in the state, the highest objectification of human freedom. Totally above the individual, the state becomes the embodiment of the Hegelian Idea, which stipulates that the final ethical end of the individual be identical with the moral, social, legal, and economic requirements of the state. The individual will be "taken up" (*aufheben*) in the mediation into these elements. The individual's choices will be devoid of passion; they will be reflective without commitment, and will tend to be "both-and" rather than "either-or." Indeed, "both-and" will become the ethical means of participation in the present age, and in the crowd.

As we observed earlier, one of Kierkegaard's most important encounters with modernism and its crowd took the form of a famous controversy with the Copenhagen newspaper *The Corsair* in 1846. This confrontation with the mass media is known as the *Corsair* affair. The weekly was owned and edited by one Aaron Goldschmidt, who was in fact a casual admirer of Kierkegaard. But under the stance of a popular egalitarian liberalism, his weekly had come to be an agent of ridicule for tradition, authority, or individuality, including derision of the upper classes in Denmark. The affair started when the critical reviewer P.L. Møller made some adverse references to Kierkegaard's *Stages on Life's Way* (1845), supposedly because it contained philosophical views in a publication that nominally was literary. Kierkegaard replied to this charge through the newspaper *Fatherland* by taking exception to Møller's claim, and by associating him with *The Corsair*. Writing under the pseudonym of "Frater Taciturnus," Kierkegaard accused *The Corsair* of a "corrupt cleverness" that should be ignored in literature, "as a prostitute should be ignored in society." Previous to this situation *The Corsair* had granted Kierkegaard respect under Goldschmidt's editorship. Now in spite of that tolerance Kierkegaard challenged Goldschmidt to include him in the paper's list of local persons whom it subjected to ridicule. Kierkegaard was then publicly counterattacked by *The Corsair* and held up to public derision. After this even the street children called him "old man either-or." He became a laughing-stock for the local public, and this even further distanced him from the crowd. At the height of the *Corsair* controversy he had completed his attack on Hegelianism in his *Postscript*, and he had just finished his *Philosophical Fragments*. The *Corsair* affair became an important element in Kierkegaard's review of Mrs. Gyllembourg's *Two Ages* in the months of January and February, 1846.

Kierkegaard's attack on *The Corsair* was in part at least a reflection of his belief that the press media of the present are linked to the crowd as the master of society. The affair focused Kierkegaard's attention in his *Two Ages* on mass democracy through an examination of the existential and moral significance of the press. Here the relation of the mass media to the crowd was raised as a specific philosophical issue for the first time. While it is true that the question of relating the masses and the press is as old as Montaigne, Pascal, and Goethe, yet the first delineation and extended philosophical critique of what has come to be the mass media appeared in the *Two Ages*. He began here a critique of modernity that would continue even into the environment of post-modernity.

The contemporary press media are for him guilty of "a cowardly secular-mindedness" that has enabled the crowd to become a tyrant and a norm of anonymous public approval. Journalism, he thought, must be revealed and criticized as a "corrupting sophism."[9] Not only does the popular press fail to enhance individual or group existence; it does not even urge the reader to knowledge or moral improvement. In this sense the press was among the sources for Kierkegaard's *contemptus mundi*. Kierkegaard had hoped that his attack on *The Corsair* would stimulate Goldschmidt to transcend the standards of mass journalism; yet he finally came to believe that presses like *The Corsair* will not distinguish between the printing of news

and "ignorant meddlesomeness"; in fact, a frequent tendency
of the media is to generate disharmony and hostility in society.
But the passions that the media arouse have no relation to the
"passion" that Kierkegaard requires of the individual for his or
her final commitment. The media are in the service of the
crowd and want to substitute the inessential and the external
for the inwardness that is the possession of Kierkegaard's
authentic individual. For Kierkegaard the whole question of
individuality is at risk in the implications of the *Corsair* affair.
The Corsair was a representative organ of the crowd, anonymous and external, and he knew it would vilify any individual
who would seek to counteract it. Media like *The Corsair* tend
also to destroy any author whose work has a relevance either to
inwardness or individuality. While Kierkegaard recognized that
the press is always at the service of profit, he did not believe
that capitalism alone could explain its influence and significance. The crowd and its media are the result of the unique
historical and sociological conditions of the present age. But
what are these conditions and how were they reflected in the
Corsair affair?

Kierkegaard scholars have long noted that Kierkegaard's
study of the "present age" is one which was later paralleled and
continued by the German sociologist Ferdinand Tönnies (1855-
1936) in his *Gemeinschaft und Gesellschaft* (in English translation
Community and Society, 1957). This study, relevant to Kierkegaard's work, was an analysis of the distinction between a social
order which was characterized by a community (*Gemeinschaft*) of
spontaneous feudal groupings with face-to-face relationships,
and *Gesellschaft*, the society of the present age of individualism,
competition, and legally mediated economic relationships
between individuals. This *Gesellschaft* social order came into
being with the rise of early modern capitalism and was subsequently identified with relations modeled after patterns of self-
interest and atomized individuation. In contrast to the fixed
and traditional roles of feudal society, individuals in the
contemporary *Gesellschaft* social order are so separated and
isolated that each exists in a state of tension and competition
with the other. Such a situation is characteristic of a society that
is devoted to the advance of wealth and power through private

property and competitive economic relations. The *Gesellschaft* social order represents a nearly complete triumph over the previous feudal communalism of the middle ages, and it has come to symbolize the dominant form of contemporary social, moral, and economic existence.

For Kierkegaard, though he did not use the term, the *Gesellschaft* social order is a radically inadequate ground for the attainment of man's final end or even for the attainment of the ethical stage of existence. The media and even the contemporary Christian church have reified this *Gesellschaft* order by accepting the bourgeois secularism, passionlessness, domineering envy of money and possessions, and outwardness of the numerical public. The press thrives upon the principle of the isolated individual, in which persons are thrown into economic conflict with all others in a posture of universal competition. Here the individual is socialized only through his participation in what Thomas Carlyle called "the cash nexus." Such *Gesellschaft* economics becomes a sort of "divinized power" of the anonymous social order which avoids moral or spiritual responsibility. It attempts to escape blame for any defeat and accept credit for any victory. Likewise, such a socio-economic condition promotes the anonymity of the individual. This loss of self destroys the rewards or meaning of the competitive economic struggle in which he or she is trapped, and it negates his or her possibilities of attaining an ethical or religious existence.

The press in this situation is the very embodiment of anonymous power in the age of abstraction. The journalist attempts to sanctify for his "gallery public" current customs, beliefs, fashions, and ideologies. Himself an irresponsible and anonymous agent with respect to individuality, the journalist can appear as the concrete and actual voice of public opinion. The press stands for nobody yet appears to stand for everybody. This is why for Kierkegaard there are not ten people in a generation who are much afraid of having an incorrect opinion, but millions are afraid of standing against the press even with a correct opinion. While the great need of the present age is to reform the crowd through the power of the press, in actual practice "the lowest depth before God" is assumed by journalism. The crowd fears its own reformation, so it assigns the task of reforming the world to politics and the press, not to itself; the possibilities of the individual, then, tend to be restricted to political or media events. And in carrying out its assignment of taking up the individual's possibilities the press possesses no conscience. The formulation of modern society has been relegated to politics and the media, thereby creating a "deep misfortune" of "unhappy objectivity," for the "I" has become a mere object, and personal inwardness is lost. This misfortune is in part the result of the media's nullification of the either-or possibilities that stand before the individual in either ethical or religious orientation. For example, whereas formerly the person had to decide either to be concerned with salvation or not, now we all tend to fit the common mould of opinion that everyone and everything is right, and whatever I do is acceptable, so long as it's not a crime. The either-or possibilities of the individual have become the unitary reality of the crowd; the crowd has collapsed all possibilities into itself, excluding the validity of the individual who does not realize himself or herself within its confines.

(D) Mass Relationships and the Christian Mission

Our final end-goal, according to Kierkegaard, is to become a single one in a relationship to the eternal. This Kierkegaardian individual (*den Enkelte*) is one who has actualized the stages of life, and has become aware of the inwardness that perfects itself through the eternal.[10] Part of Kierkegaard's life-work was to ask about the condition of the individual and of the Christian of the present age. He concluded that the Christian of the present age is not only in but of the crowd; the individual has been largely transformed into a numerical abstraction, a specimen of what he or she has "in common" with the crowd. The crowd acts as a mediating agent which identifies our final end with itself; the crowd or public becomes our sole point of reference. All our relationships, eternal and secular, tend to be mass relations, which lack the separating power of inwardness. With inwardness gone, the individual's self-relation by reference to the eternal is removed. Individuals are left only to the rude externality of abstract categories, such as progress, equality, envy, money, and the media. By relating to such categories, the individual's inwardness is dimmed down by external *Gesellschaft* society. For the person the individuating factor of inwardness tends to give way to the public's chatter or gossip. Talking becomes a sort of mid-ground between individual inwardness and the crowd, and the distinction between public and private is further mediated. Because it wants to be "outward," talk usually refers to those definite actions, beliefs, and facts by which the individual can exhibit the most public information. Such talk attempts to refer only to those principles or exhortations upon which anyone in the crowd could act. As a public entity talk does not know or recognize contradiction, and its superficiality is always welcomed by the crowd. In making talk the dominant form of public life, the individual abandons all inwardness. A "rabble barbarism" arranges the world in accord with what "they say" (*das Man*). *Das Man* refers here to the collective of insubstantial individuals who have abandoned the concrete individuation of authentic personhood.

It is at this point that the crowd will tend to believe that politics is the last concretion, the last authentic vocation. But Kierkegaard believed that in *New Testament* Christianity politics was not recognized as a significant *telos* for the Christian individual. The early Christians and the Church Fathers tended to see politics as part of the "world system"; politics was considered a false mediation between the temporal and the eternal, and as such it was a constant temptation to the crowd of that day. Yet the Christians of the modern age are significantly part of both politics and its servant, the crowd. Contemporary Christians have forgotten or repressed the form of life demanded by the *New Testament*; they are in danger of surrendering the eternal to politics, mass culture, science, money, or envy. All of these secular forms, especially politics, may be subsumed under the guise of "progress," and this same "progress" can quickly become associated with such a secular humanistic abstraction as "pure humanity." For the modern age such a secular abstraction has tended to become the highest moral vision. But the ideology of "progress" or "pure humanity" is usually the disguised attempt to fabricate a secular equality among abstract individuals. Such an abstraction will then tend to replace the *New Testa-*

ment assertion of the authentic equality of all individuals before God. The secular equality of the mass is a concept that will never relate to any but partisan political visions.

Part of Kierkegaard's purpose in his *Two Ages*, and part of his mission generally, was to correct the massification of the individual by showing that such reflective abstractions as "pure humanity" and "equality" are not moral or spiritual constructions, but political ones. They are merely the abstract universals which divest the truly authentic possibilities of the individual. The most important of these possibilities is the relation of the individual to the eternal in faith as the culmination of life's stages. This final realization, the one proper to the individuation of the person, is the opposite of the political dispersion of the individual into the abstractions of pure humanity and equality. Against these, our possibilities in Christ become for Kierkegaard our completed being, our perfected individual existence. Christ's life was a work of love, and his actions were prescriptive for the final ends of the individual. He enjoined that we must love our neighbor as ourselves, and not replace this love with the secular abstractions of the crowd. In this respect Kierkegaard believed that contemporary Christianity has significantly given way to the secularization of the crowd. The supremacy of the Christian individual should be our most important concern, but the crowd has only contempt for the individual, and its power of corruption is "greater than any vice." The supremacy of the individual implies that he or she is never morally or spiritually perfected by the crowd. The individual must come to understand that while the social uplifters would seem to perfect the progress of the individual, the leveling of the present age only renders the plight of the individual more desperate. Leveling obscures the fact that our ultimate help does not come from the crowd, but from individual faith and commitment.

For Kierkegaard the criteria of the person's authentic Christian individuation may be outlined as follows. First, the person must stand apart from the crowd's capriciousness and coercion. Secondly, the individual must attempt to deliver other individuals from the self-deception of the crowd. The status of the individual is "akin to Deity," and the individual alone is capable of receiving and sharing the truth. All communication of the final truth must be addressed to and by the person and never the crowd. It is the individual and never the mass which is edified, and edification is always dependent upon the eternal.[11] Thirdly, we must practice the inward mode of existence, and the category of inwardness must be both practiced and preached in the modern age. In a desperate age we may hope for the coming of a "single one" who will proclaim the individual to the crowd; this event may happen even though nobody seems to want "that exhausted thing," the individual. The authentic witness of the individual is especially necessary, for Kierkegaard, because persons of the present age have become "ground smooth as a pebble" and have failed in both their individuation and their relation to God. When we have lost our orientation to this final *telos*, then for Kierkegaard our decline into the mass is inevitable.

Christ is the final truth of the individual and is the source which perfects individuation in the person. But Kierkegaard warned that Christian individuation depends significantly upon the example and martyrdom of select Christian individuals. Martyrs need not be special or gifted individuals, but they require Grace to show their contemporaries what they lack, i.e., the individuation of authentic Christians. But even a martyr's power is limited, for Kierkegaard further warned us that neither the martyr not the individual can save an age; rather, he or she "can only express that it is foundering." A martyr for Kierkegaard is the opposite of the "hero" that the crowd usually admires, for the modern "hero" is ambiguous and does not possess authority. The "hero" tends to exist for the crowd, and it is a "diabolical leveling" that usually allows the hero and his crowd to be efficacious. The authentic alternative either to the hero or to leveling is the martyrdom of the witnessing individual who not only addresses the masses but is able to step back from the crowd into inwardness. Inwardness "knows no public"; and it is only in the martyr's suffering act that the individual can provide an indirect help to the present age. In his conflicts with both the church and *The Corsair* Kierkegaard became this person: he attempted to be more than the Christian intellectual and polemicist; he attempted to be the "one thing needful," the martyr in critical ministration to his age. It is only under desperate conditions that the unredeemed world will make use of men like him. The martyr alone is able to stand against his age and minister to its authentic ends. And this Kierkegaard became.

(E) The Individual and the Christian Community

Theologians as varied as Richard Niebuhr and Martin Buber have claimed that Kierkegaard's individualism led him to an ultra-conservative and anti-communal point of view. This criticism seems to suggest that Kierkegaard was too unconcerned with the world, and that he understood the community as a lower category than that of the individual. Such interpretations of Kierkegaard had also been advanced in the nineteenth century by Hans Martensen, Kierkegaard's teacher and the primate of the Danish church. From such judgments it would seem to follow that his thought adds little or nothing to our grasp of communal existence. Yet these judgments do not sufficiently comprehend Kierkegaard's actual position. Kierkegaard never perceived personal individuation as the sole spiritual good, nor did he understand the individual's personal existence in a socio-political vacuum. He never considered individuality or inwardness apart from the wider context of communal well-being. While it is not difficult to assume from such texts as the *Postscript* that his categories of inwardness and subjectivity reveal a devaluation of both community and human sociality, this devaluation was not his intent.

Kierkegaard's critique of the crowd and his advocacy of the individual always presupposed Christian community. In such a community the eternal becomes the ground of individual well-being and the basis of human relationships in *agape*. The ideal communal status requires that the individual relate to the other through the mediation of divine love. Our relation to the eternal, then, is partly social, and our completed individuality is communally related. Ideally the individual should never be without such a community, but in the present age it must remain an ideal of faith. Itself a secularized mass, the present Danish church was for Kierkegaard an inadequate medium to this end. But even the ideal of the community is not a concrete possibility without a prior attack on the hegemony of the crowd. The crowd imagines itself the final community, a status into which all must fit and none can avoid. Kierkegaard questioned this assumption. It is this questioning of his, rather than his relatively undeveloped position on the Christian community, that is crucial here. No conception of Christian community can be adequate without a critical thesis on the crowd, and this is perhaps Kierkegaard's greatest contribution to the idea of community.

While the mass acts to counteract the individual's relation to the eternal, and while the present age would nullify the eternal in the individual, Kierkegaard contended that after the present has passed, history will orient itself to the religious community. In this stage of history the individual will be primarily related to God and only secondarily to the community. The reformation of the individual will be based not on political or social equality but on the equality of the individual before God. In this future state the cohesiveness of the community will arise from Christian individuation, and because of this, the individual will remain qualitatively higher than the community. Yet in this future polity individuals will be related to their neighbors in works of love. The individual in the Christian community will be fulfilled in a new way, in his or her relation both to the other and to God through divine love.

(F) The Crowd is Despair

The present age, the age of the crowd, is possessed by secular enthusiasms which are in part quasi-religious. These are equality, progress, and material possessions generated by envy. Kierkegaard believed that these secular obsessions neither humanize nor save individuals, but only serve to release them from the demands of spirit and religious vocation. The crowd seeks to find release from the demands of truth and goodness, possessing no competency in either; nor does it possess either responsibility or virtue. In spite of these lacks, the contemporary individual still continues to assume that the crowd is the major trans-personal point of reference. In this situation it will appear to the individual that his or her humanity can be attained only through economic amelioration, social status, or such rituals of mass society as education, career, the military, and marriage or divorce. Kierkegaard's mission was in part the attempt to provide an alternative to such rituals and to unsocialize the individual and un-deify mass society. From his earliest writings on Socrates through his experiences with *The Corsair* and the Danish church, Kierkegaard urged the individual to refuse to equate personal virtue or his or her final *telos* with "normative socialization."[12] Such a refusal is crucial for the attempt of the individual to grasp the eternal in the flux of society and history. But such an orientation is a viable option only for that individual who has been significantly de-socialized from the cemented roles of mass society. Kierkegaard hoped to contribute to this end through his Christian vocation in writing, through his analysis of the crowd, and through his critique of Hegel.

It was vital to Kierkegaard that he be able to overcome the mediation that Hegel had constructed between the secular and the Absolute, the individual and the social. He believed that both of these mediations have been enshrined in the institutions of mass society, and they have acted as impairments to both Christianity and the de-secularization of society. Further, Kierkegaard also held that the great issue of his life was the antagonism between him and Hegelianism on the theological issue of apotheosis versus incarnation, i.e., the question whether human beings fulfill their final end through historical self-transcendence, or whether they achieve their final end by relating to the incarnation of Christ, who appears in history from the transcendent and eternal. In other words, will our final end be comprehended under the category of social-moral evolution and secular historicity of the Hegelian version, or will it be seen as a transcendent gift of Grace, which is thrown into our human condition "like a stone" from a divinely transcendent source? For Kierkegaard individuals possess a choice here. Either they place their ultimate hope in society and the historical process as the proper universals of human life, or they attempt to realize their final end through the authentic individuation of the person through the leap of faith. The first of

these, the Hegelian alternative, will involve the risk of conduct-
ing the individual into the furtherance of mass culture and pos-
sibly totalitarianism. In the second alternative, the "single one"
who risks the life of faith will resist the categories of "humanity"
and "equality" as abstract substitutes for the authentic Christian
community. Also in taking the second alternative, the individual
will realize that there is a refuge from the "dizziness" of mass
humanity only in the religious life. Kierkegaard even noted that
this "dizziness" of the mass may prompt the individual to the
leap of faith as leveling advances and nearly consumes the individual. In this state the individual may come to realize that the
crowd seeks to become an egalitarian mass, not out of virtue,
but from the belief that such a conformity will "pare down" the
other and reduce our fear. The Christian individual must come
to the realization that authentic equality is never abstract or
impersonal, as in the crowd, but is the honoring of every person in the truth, i.e., in the love of God and of one's neighbor
as oneself. Here is the realization of true equality, and all who
love their neighbor as themselves reverence this equality as the
truth. In this sense equality in faith is not the mass man, but an
achievement of the individual who has related to the eternal,
and, through the eternal, to the community of faith.

For Kierkegaard the growth of the egalitarian mass in the
present age has an important relation to the presence of anxiety and despair in both the individual and the crowd. He wrote
of both of these states in *The Concept of Dread* (1844), where he
described a pervasive anxiety which is the product of the individual's feeling of two contrary inner states: attraction and
repulsion. The individual in this state feels a contradiction
between an attraction to freedom and a dread of the possibilities that freedom brings. Kierkegaard exemplified this state in
the example of Adam. Adam was prohibited the fruit of the tree
of knowledge of good and evil under the punishment of death;
but this prohibition awoke in him the possibility of freedom. He
here realized that he was able or "free" to sin by violating the
commandment. He was at once attracted to the sin yet repulsed
by it and its prohibition. At once he experienced dread and
attraction for the same state. Attracted by the unknown state of
sin, which was nevertheless a threat to his security, Adam knew

the torn-apart-ness of dread. For Kierkegaard this same dread
or anxiety is generated by the individual's relation to the crowd.
Feeling at once attracted by the crowd's apparent inclusiveness
and security, yet lost in the crowd's abstraction and out-of-
himself-ness, the individual may fall into a secular despair. This
despair will take the form of a refusal or abandonment of the
individual's sense of personal possibility. Self-transcendence will
be rejected for the sense in the individual that "nothing can be
done," either as a person or as a mass.

In *The Sickness unto Death* (1849) Kierkegaard wrote under a
pseudonym to reveal the experience of despair by a "no one,"
an anonymous writer who would relate the Christian message
to a mass which was itself in secret despair. He wrote as one
who had personally experienced both despair and dread, conditions which were manifest in his deep sense of separation from
the eternal ground of his being. Despair was for him "the sickness unto death." Both the individual and the crowd always
possess the potential for despair, caused by their failure to
relate to the final ground, the eternal, which establishes their
fullest individuation, their freedom.

When the individual misses the eternal, he or she may fall
into what Kierkegaard called "infinite despair." But there is also
a despair which results from our misrelation to the mass, and
this is "the despair of finitude." Here the individual feels a lack
of possibility for a personal connection with the dominant
group or crowd. This is the despair that is common to the individual in mass society, and one of the chief pathologies of the
present age. The individual experiences a loss of confidence, a
disruption of the self from one of its essential possibilities.
When the individual lacks confidence, or when there is the
attempt to substitute for inwardness the abstract order of the
"public," then the individual's despair in mass society seems
assured. Further, if the individual attempts along with the
crowd to fabricate the secular order into an image of the
eternal, then the crowd has again become untruth. Such
untruth is really the confusion between the secular and the
eternal. This surrogate secular divinity has become the equation
of all human possibilities for self-transcendence with the total
secular arrangement of society. Any possibilities besides this

social arrangement are either forgotten or ignored, and the life of faith is dimmed in both the individual and the group. It was to counteract this despair, a despair from which there seems to be no exit, that Kierkegaard devoted his life.

PART TWO

MARTIN HEIDEGGER
AND
FRIEDRICH NIETZSCHE

Chapter Three

Heidegger's Ontological Formulation of *Das Man*

(A) Background

Martin Heidegger was born September 26, 1889, in Messkirch in the Black Forest area of Germany. He was of peasant origins and his father was a sexton in the local Catholic Church. This rural and Christian background would later reveal itself in his conception of the nature of human individuation in the techno-massification of the twentieth century. He had considered the Catholic priesthood as his vocation, and he briefly attended Jesuit seminary before his entrance into the University of Freiburg in 1909. Here he took up the study of theology and philosophy. He had been influenced previously by Franz Brentano's (1838-1907) *Vom der mannigfachen Bedeutung des Seienden bei Aristoteles* (1862) (*On the Manifold Meaning of Being According to Aristotle*). For Heidegger, Aristotle would remain the *fons et origo* of the existential thinking which would later emerge in German thought with the translation of Kierkegaard's works.[1] His 1914 doctoral dissertation was entitled *Die Lehre vom Urteil im Psychologismus* ("The Doctrine of Judgment in Psychologism"). It was an examination of the objectivity and general validity (*Allgemeingültigkeit*) that is philosophically required of all psychological judgments upon the discursive nature of human consciousness. Heidegger then became a student of the neokantian philosopher Heinrich Rickert (1863-1936). But the epistemological emphasis of neokantianism in this thinker failed to hold his philosophical interest after 1912, because the young Heidegger believed that Rickert's movement had neglected the ontological questions that had been raised in Aristotle's thought. His 1916 *Habilitation* essay, in which Heidegger examined John Duns Scotus' (c. 1300) doctrine of judgment and categories, revealed the influence of Edmund Husserl's (1859-1938) *Logical Investigations.* Heidegger became Husserl's assistant at Freiburg after he had seen service in World War I. But even before this period he had shown a strong interest in the work of Wilhelm Dilthey (1833-1911), whose *Lebensphilosophie* he saw as a viable alternative to Husserl's rationalism and a-historical phenomenology. Heidegger took a leave from Freiburg for the University of Marburg, where he taught until 1928. There he became a friend of the Protestant theologians Rudolf Bultmann and Paul Tillich, and the philosophers Max Scheler and Karl Jaspers. At this time he built his cabin retreat in Todnauberg in the Black Forest, where he completed the first half of his *Being and Time* (1927) for Husserl's *Yearbook for Philosophy and Phenomenological Research.* With the publication of this work Heidegger would emerge as Germany's leading philosopher. Hannah Arendt, one of his students at the time, reported that there spread through Germany a rumor that a "hidden king" had appeared in modern thought.

Heidegger was a member of the National Socialist Party when he was appointed Rector of the University of Freiburg. At first he believed that the party's policies would turn Germany from the technicity and modernism of contemporary Europe, Russia, and America. He shortly resigned his rectorship at the university after he became disillusioned with the Nazi movement. For the six-year period of the Allied occupation he was forbidden to teach at Freiburg, until 1951. Working at his retreat in the Black Forest, where he received visitors from all over the world, he would write and think as an independent scholar and he would also continue his earlier study of the poet Friedrich Hölderlin (1770-1843). At his death in 1976 he was given Christian burial next to his parents in the Messkirch Cemetery. A complete edition of his work is presently being published by the house of Vittorio Klostermann in Frankfurt, appearing in four parts: (1) Published Writings from 1914-1970; (2) Lecture Courses from 1923-1944; (3) Unpublished Work from 1919-1967; (4) Notes, Papers, etc. The project will come to some fifty-five volumes.

We have noted that Heidegger was Husserl's assistant from 1920-1923, and there were aspects of Husserl's method and doctrine that informed Heidegger's own thought. In Husserl's *Logical Investigations* (1900-1901) phenomenology was defined as the description of the contents of consciousness or our immediate lived experience (*Erlebnis*). Such phenomenological description is possible when we have returned to the "things themselves," by means of the method of phenomenological "seeing" that claims priority to the "natural standpoint" of the empirical sciences. In his *Ideen zu einer reinen Phänomenologie* (Halle, 1913) (*Idea of a Pure Phenomenology*), Husserl presented phenomenology as the general philosophical method for the inquiry into all meaning. Here it was maintained that all that can exist for us is a correlate of consciousness. The nature of consciousness is only to be found in what his teacher Franz Brentano (1838-1907) had designated as the intentionality (*Intentionalität*) of mental life. This term meant to point to the fact that our consciousness is always "of" or "about" that which it intends. But in addition to this intentional feature of consciousness, Husserl postulated the existence of the transcendental ego, that experiential center which bestows universal meaning upon all that exists. This transcendental realm for Husserl is the proper object of all philosophical reflection. Husserl's work culminated in *The Crisis of European Science and Transcendental Phenomenology* (1936). Here he developed the thesis of intersubjectivity in historical time, and phenomenology was extended beyond the previous description of the transcendental ego to a life world (*Lebenswelt*) that exists prior to any cultural or scientific thematization.

Heidegger, like Husserl, understood phenomenology from the standpoint of a pretheoretical orientation to primordial human existence, which he designated as *Dasein* (human Being). The method of his inquiry is phenomenological, and by this term he understood in his *Being and Time* the description of that which discloses itself in the immediacy of itself.[2] The term φαινόμενον is that which can disclose itself through itself as that which it is. Phenomenological science here sets for itself the goal of the revelation of the structure and content of Dasein.

Yet Heidegger later claimed that his mentor's thought was derived from Descartes and Kant, not Dilthey; and for this reason neither the radical reality nor the historicality of human life nor even Being itself was adequately comprehended in Husserl's thought.[3] Heidegger did not understand human Being as a Husserlean transcendental ego. He saw human nature as temporal, finite, and grounded in care. His *Being and Time* (1927) provided an interpretation of the meaning of human Being through the examination of the ontological structures that compose it. Such an interpretation, he thought, has philosophical priority over both Husserl's absolute ego and the epistemological concerns of the Western tradition since Descartes. For Heidegger it is Being as such (*Sein*) which is the central yet presently forgotten issue of philosophy, and the question of human Being's historical nature is the preliminary issue of the question of Being itself. His quest was more than a factical science of philosophical anthropology; it was fundamental ontology.

Heidegger announced his general goal in his subtitle in Part One of *Being and Time* as "The Interpretation of Dasein in Terms of Temporality, and the Explication of Time as the Transcendental Horizon for the Question of Being." He never completed a second half of *Being and Time,* and his published volume composes only the two divisions "Preparatory Fundamental Analysis of Dasein" and "Dasein and Temporality." Both of these sections are an attempt to reveal that human existence is an event that always presupposes the presence (*Anwesen*) of Being. The Greeks had understood this presence as that by which existent beings become revealed as what they are. But the subsequent philosophical tradition attempted to comprehend Being only in terms of those beings or entities-that-are (*Seiendes*). As a result of such a misinterpretation, the question of the meaning of Being itself has been progressively forgotten and repressed in the West since the time of Plato and Aristotle.

In opposition to this Western neglect, Heidegger asserted that human Being is always the "there-being" or the place of openness where Being happens; that human Being always lives with the awareness, however vague, that it is grounded in Being, which is the ultimate condition of all beings that exist.[4] Authentic philosophical thought must distinguish the so-called "ontological difference" between Being as such and the being-which-is-at-hand; to understand the meaning of Being through the examination of our human Being (Dasein) should be prior to an attempt of the sciences to objectify thinking through the explanation of things-that-are. The problem of philosophy is not factual examinations or explanations after the models of science or epistemology, but the interrogation of the Being which is most proximate to us, our own. So the West must again pose the central question of philosophy: "What does it mean to be?" Humanity must preserve a "vigilance for Being" (*Wachterschaft des Seins*), for such vigilance alone will decide the fate of humanity on Earth. Heidegger believed that in his *Being and Time* he had re-inaugurated the search for the meaning of Being in the horizon of time and from the point of view of the Being (Dasein) whose interiority is most proximate to us. He addressed this fundamental, urgent, ontological question through a delineation of those existential features that Dasein exhibits as its necessary and immediate components. It is to these features that we must now turn.

(B) The Existential Structures of Individual and Social Human Being

Heidegger's *Being and Time* was in significant part the attempt to reveal the characteristics of human Being (Dasein) through those universal existential structures that inform its everyday existence. While Heidegger's thought was always directed to the quest for Being itself (*Sein*), his analysis, in the phenomenological tradition, was initially directed to human Being. Dasein is that entity which alone is capable of inquiring into its own Being, of wondering about its own existence. The meaning of existence can be relevant only for one who first asks about the existence which is most proximate to him or her; even to raise the question of the meaning of Being, one must already possess a vague knowledge of Being in the existence that he or she is. Heidegger attempted to reveal those universal structures or

Existentials of the a priori ways of our being that allow us to become aware of Being in the first place. He designated as the Existential Analytic the collection of those ontological characteristics of human Being in everyday existence which distinguish it from the Being of such entities as objects-at-hand, the objects of the special sciences which Heidegger called ontical sciences. We must now selectively examine some of the most relevant Existentials which are central both to Heidegger's project and to our own inquiry into *das Man*.

The most fundamental existential component of our existence Heidegger called our Being-in-the-world (*In-der-Welt-sein*). More than the fact that we live on the earth, this "world" existential is meant to indicate that we are always in circumstances to which we must orient our existence. Our Being-in-the-world is always a subject-object relationship that no scepticism about the external world can cancel. The "naturalistic attitude" of empirical science that the universe enjoys a real and independent status apart from that human Being-in-the-world is now deemed impossible. Being-in-the-world is the ground for our experience of nature and history. Further, Dasein exists in constant concern or Care for its worldly status. Dasein's Being-in-the-world means that entities always exist for it as objects-to-hand for Dasein's uses and possibilities. This at-handedness (*Vorhandenheit*) of the world signifies that entities are never neutral but are functionally related to all the projects, thoughts, and concerns of Dasein. In this sense the at-handedness of the world is a constant feature of our existence.

A second Existential of Dasein is understanding (*Verstehen*). Heidegger used the term to mean that human existence is open to the future in such a way that it casts a tendential structure ahead of itself as part of its Being. This structure is Dasein's apprehension of its own possibilities. In other words, Dasein is aware of the structure of its able-to-be-ness, for it can anticipate its future, or graduate itself to a new status, through what Heidegger termed "projection" (*Entwurf*). By projective anticipation Dasein opens up its possibilities of place, action, creations, and meanings in its Being-in-the-world. Dasein's projective able-to-be-ness is the structured manner by which it attempts to achieve control over its future existence from the standpoint of the present. These possibilities of existence are our own-most possessions, possessions about which we must care as we advance in time.

Meaning (*Sinn*) is Heidegger's third Existential, by which Dasein incorporates new elements of the world into those awarenesses and projects that it already possesses. In order to have meaning, something must have a relevance to Dasein's past and its possibilities. If one of Dasein's new possibilities possesses a determinate relation to a previous possibility, i.e., if it "fits" into a context of previously sedimented projections, then this new possibility of Dasein possesses both a functional and contextual significance; it joins (along with all previously confirmed and serviceable projections) the collection of meanings that have established this human Being's competence in the world. We see then that Dasein does not exist in presuppositionless and unprejudiced states, for it always brings its previous accumulations of meaning to its present and its future. For example, a facial expression is seen as something friendly or indifferent, etc., but such a "seeing" always exists in the context of previous implications that friendly or indifferent faces portend for our existence. Dasein's meanings and projections, then, are always temporal, because they have a definite reference to past, present, or future connections. Put in another way, Dasein carries its historically derived forms of life into its present world and into a future about which it must be concerned. Dasein's meaningful comportment toward its future is a central component of our radically historical nature.

Another important element is Heidegger's hermeneutic circle. This term is meant to indicate that understanding and inquiry are "circular" in the sense that the interpreter always brings to the interpretant or world-at-hand the pre-existing frames of meaning and reference which constitute the significance of such a world-at-hand. The world does not exist neutrally, or as a clear and distinct object. Instead the world must always remain an object of possible interpretation, and all interpretation is circular in its presuppositions of what something has been and what it has been projected for. Such possibilities of the interpretant exist as the criteria by which Dasein has previously arranged facts and data and assigned purposes to phenomena. Circularity implies that Dasein comes to objects in the world by casting upon them the past possibilities that were present in the previous constructions of Dasein. In other words, the manner in which we have been in time and the manner in which we conceive the future are always preconditions for the way that we come to understand something in the present. For Heidegger it is this temporal circularity that grounds the human studies generally. This circularity of understanding is rooted in the very structure of Dasein.[5]

In Division One of *Being and Time*, entitled "Care as the Being of Dasein," Heidegger asserted that the fundamental existential structure of human life is not reason, soul substance, or ego, but care (*Sorge*). Care is the fundamental earmark of human life in that all of the existentials which Heidegger developed in his book find their final ground of meaning by their integration into this structure. Care most fully reveals the nature of Dasein's existence as a whole. It possesses a three-fold structure which Heidegger called facticity (*Faktizität*), falling (*Verfallen*), and possibility (*Möglichkeit*). This three-fold structure of Care is claimed to represent the basic constitution of human existence, the deepest ground of the Existentials of Dasein. The first of Care's structures, Facticity, denotes all those elements in human existence which are simply given to us, not chosen. Facticity indicates that human Being is always in a world which it did not will or create. But this world is ours to appropriate and assimilate within the limits of finite contingency. Facticity would therefore include both the unchangeable givenness of our past and the fact that Dasein must accept and appropriate that past to our present and future. Falling, the second element of the Care structure, refers to the fact that Dasein is concerned with the present and yet is alienated and turned away from the actuality of its own world. Subsequent description of this Falling element will be developed in Part C. Possibility, the third element of Care, refers to the reality of Dasein's open future, and its anticipation in care of that future. Possibility indicates too the necessity of Dasein's decision upon a definite mode of its own future.

In Division Two of *Being and Time,* entitled "Dasein and Temporality," Heidegger asked if there is even a deeper structure or medium which makes the Care structure possible. We are then told that this structure or medium is Temporality (*Zeitlichkeit*), whose three ecstases, past, present and future, he correlated with the three existential characteristics of facticity, falling, and possibility; facticity is correlated with the past, falling with the present, and possibility with the future. In this manner, Temporality emerges as the basic characteristic of human existence, second in import only to our Being-in-the-world.

Because Dasein must decide upon its own future in a determinate way, the future is anticipated by existence as something that is always ahead of itself, a not-yet constituted possibility. When we have cast our own-most possibilities onto the future, we have authentically performed a projective resolution (*vorläufende Entschlossenheit*) upon the existence we are to become. These elements of the Care structure, then, along with the three modes of Temporality, make possible our existence and the wholeness of Dasein. Since Dasein's Care structure is thus grounded in Temporality, Temporality provides the unity of our existence, and it is only in so far as Dasein possesses the character of Temporality that it has the potentiality for being a whole, especially as it orients itself to the future. Temporality becomes the fulfillment of the Care structure and its deepest meaning. Human Being is a being in time.

Heidegger's conception of Temporality would exclude from consideration all previous metaphysical attempts to define time in terms of the movement of natural entities-at-hand. Any attempt such as that of Aristotle's to grasp time through the counting of the motion of entities has obscured the role of the primordial time revealed in the Temporality of Dasein's Care structure. We must also come to the position that what is understood as objective or world time is in fact founded in Dasein's Temporality. The objective datability of Dasein's Temporality becomes the very ground of clock time, and it is ontologically prior to it. But the attempt to equate public or objective time with Temporality itself has obscured the fundamental nature of Dasein's primal time, as especially Dasein's Historicality (*Geschichtlichkeit*), an Existential to which we must now turn.

The Existential that most authentically describes the unique manner in which humanity is in time is Historicality. This term is derived from a tradition as old as Hegel, and in it we have the notion that man is by nature a historical being. This means that we are not in time as a thing (*Innerzeitlichkeit*), but as a being which possesses past, present, and future in such a way that they compose an intersubjective world. Dasein possesses as part of its Care and Temporality structure the capacity to appropriate its own past and anticipate its future from its present, whereas a thing in public time possesses no such selfreflecting world, and its temporality consists of its movement from one "now-point" to another, its past lost with each oncoming moment, and its future a "now" which is not yet present. In historical existence Dasein is not merely in time as a public thing-to-hand, but takes time and has time as its very own-most possession. Heidegger also made here the apparently strange claim that human Being is essentially historical because of the element of futurity in its existence. The future provides not only the basis of history, but it is the primary element in human temporality. One would normally assume that it is from the past that we are historical beings, but for Heidegger it is only through Dasein's projection of its possibilities into the future that its existence displays a temporality different from a thing's. Humanity is historical not because it jumps from one now-point to a future one, but because it projects its future possibilities in such a manner that it makes them its own. Its self-conscious attainment of future possibilities makes of Dasein a historically significant Being. Historical human action signifies the projection of possibilities into the future in such a way that it composes the Being that Dasein is. For Heidegger history is the study of the humanly possible,[6] and such possibility requires the existence of the future, because Dasein projects itself from the contexts of its past and the resoluteness of its present to the possibilities of its future. In this sense human Being is *ab initio* Historicality, because it is always a temporal possibility ahead of itself, a past which it has appropriated as its own, a present from which it anticipates and projects, and a future of possibilities which it seeks to make its own.

Heidegger understood the Historicality of human Being as that which is "primarily historical," because it is the existential foundation for the "ontical" sciences of history (*Historie*). Such empirical sciences, along with their subject matter of records, artifacts, documents, creations, and actions, Heidegger designated as the "secondarily historical." The historical sciences are "secondarily historical" because they derive their meaning from the Historicality of Dasein, to whose world they belonged and were "at hand" (*Zuhandensein*) for human use. Historical science, then, is not grounded in objective fact, nor upon the aged status of an entity, nor even upon the relation between the historical knower and "objective facts." Instead historical science is grounded in a "hermeneutical situation," i.e., grounded in a world of previous significance for Dasein. In this situation the interpretant is the empirical material at hand in Dasein's world; the interpreter is the primarily historical Being who projects significant possibilities on these materials at hand. The science of history becomes possible because interpreter and interpretant share a common world; and the evidences of the past are understandable to the interpreter because he or she understands (*Verstehen*) the repeatable possibilities that belong to Dasein's world.

The word "existence" is a derivation from the Latin term *exsistere*, that which "stands out" from itself in transcendence toward its possibilities. Dasein's existence, unlike objects-at-hand, is always an orientation to a world. It is a "being there" (*Da-sein*) in a world to which it must orient itself, and from which it can never escape or separate itself. It is from this existential basis that Heidegger posed the problem of the self under the heading of "the who of Dasein," the existence that stands out from its ownness and which is expressed by the personal pronoun "I."[7] Such an "I" appropriates its own past, belongs to itself in the present, and anticipates its own future. Dasein's existence is always in time, and it must accept as its ownness the actual temporal situations into which it has been thrown (*Geworfenheit*), be these its race, sex, genetic inheritance, or its sociohistorical situations. Dasein must always be in some particular situation or condition that is not chosen, and these unchosen aspects of our existence, as we have seen, Heidegger designated as the Facticity of human Being. Yet human Being is already aware, at least implicitly, of what it means to be, and of what it means to become. Heidegger considered in his *Being and Time* how these means of existence are possible at all, and he made it apparent how Dasein's possibilities become definite. Definiteness emerges as Dasein projects itself upon something in terms of what it wants to be understood "as." This is accomplished when Dasein assigns to something a use or purpose. These projections are grounded in a so-called fore-having (*Vorhabe*). Here he meant that in our interpretation of the world we always take to an object a previous expectation of it in terms of some specific function or purpose; this expectation of use is our fore-having of it. A thing's significance depends upon the ends which Dasein has imparted to it. Meaning is not simply a matter of how we stipulate the use of words; meaning is derived from the possibilities of Dasein. These possibilities are made explicit in terms of use, relations, and pre-conception. Meaning here becomes the conditions under which human Being will do something definite in existence.

That which Dasein utilizes for a specific purpose in the world is "equipment," and all equipment must "fit" the systems of society's uses. Such societal uses are themselves part of the sociohistorical traditions of Dasein. Dasein relates to this equipment in circumspection and concern, for "equipmentality" or usefulness always exists in the nexus of Care. In addition, Dasein must become what it is through the assumptions of social practices, roles, and norms that are presupposed in our Being-with others (*Mitsein*). In this sense, Dasein interprets itself, at least in large part, as a "one," a "they," or an "anybody" with whom it could exchange parts or become a significant part. This possibility of ourselves as "significant others" is called *das Man*. This means that we are largely given to ourselves through the appropriation of what the sociohistorical background of our present does, expects, or assumes as normal. We are pregiven to ourselves socially as "with others." Heidegger defined the *das Man* Existential as the disclosedness of the They, as a way of interpreting the social possibilities against the background significance of everyday Dasein.[8] At its deepest being, Dasein is social, and "with others" in terms of the roles, expectations, and uses that it presupposes of others and lives out in itself. In the *Being and Time* Heidegger asked how Dasein is socially and historically intelligible to itself, and he replied that the greatest source of our intersubjective intelligibility in our Being-in-the-world is the "one," "they," or "anybody" Existential (*das Man*). The primary manner by which we are given to ourselves is *das Man*. We come to the conclusion that the "who of Dasein," its self, is primarily and for the most part the sociality of our Being-with. We are primarily a Being-in-the-world, and the world exists for us significantly as a public sociality through which we become definite to ourselves and others. We must now turn to a closer examination of this "anybody" self.

(C) Humanity as "Anybody" (*das Man*)

We have seen at this point that Care allied with time is the unifying structure behind the various modes of Dasein's existence. It is in Care that we find the totality of Dasein's ontological wholeness as the Being that it is.[9] In his clarification of this wholeness in Division I, Chapter IV, Sections 25-27 of his *Being and Time*, Heidegger raised the crucial question of the "who of Dasein." This is entitled "Being-in-the-World as Being-With and Being-One's-Self. The 'They.'" Here he addressed the identity of the self in terms of the everyday nature of Dasein. He also posed the possibility that this everyday nature may not be the "I-myself." Is it possible, he asked, that the self or the "I," a term which suggests complete individuation, may be in its everyday existence a public or social entity? Is the "who of Dasein" in fact a Being-in-the-world which understands itself as a sort of Being-with-others as a social commonality? Heidegger answered these questions in the affirmative. Our Being-in-the-world is not to be understood as a single, private who, an "I" over against all others. Instead, Heidegger explained how we are specifically in the world by reference to the Existential Being-with (*Mitsein*). This Existential he examined in the context of the previously posed question of the "who of Dasein." Philosophy has previously addressed the issue of this "who" as spirit, soul, ego, or privated inner self. Yet we still remain in basic unclarity with respect to the problem of the self. Further, Heidegger believed that all of the problems of philosophy require an elucidation of the nature of the "who" of Dasein. Not only is a private and unique self of Dasein not a fundamental notion, but Dasein can never be understood as an individuated ego which joins itself to others in the formation of society. His Existential Being-with (*Mitsein*) is his expression for the philosophical position that human Being is a priori in a world with others; that it possesses from the beginning a public dimension that is not only inter-subjective but constitutive of its very Being.

In the Existentials of Being-in-the-world and Being-with is grounded the mode of everyday Being-oneself (*Selbstsein*). Heidegger here meant to show that everyday Dasein lives largely in a mode that is not simply an "I-myself," and the "I-myself" can never serve as the starting point of any adequate analysis of Dasein, for an isolated, encapsulated subject is a fiction. Dasein exists for the most part in its everydayness so as to be indistinguishable from that which is not simply an "I-myself," but an "anybody." It is from the beginning a sociality in the world, an available-ness to others, and others to it.[10] This "Being-with" indicates that Dasein exists to others in a publicly encounterable world of common meanings, languages, prac-tices, and manipulations that can never be understood by sole reference to an "I-myself ego," but only with reference to the fact that the common encountering of a common world is part of what is meant by Dasein's a priori possibilities.[11] Whether we deal with the expectations normally posited of such public equipment as a steering wheel or a natural language, human Being understands in part how it is in the world by reference to a world that an "anybody" (*das Man*) can appropriate, use, and make relevant to its existence. This aspect of Dasein is its public nature. The equipments, uses, languages, social expectations, and norms of public Dasein are what Dasein can expect to be the possessions of others in public encounterability. They are our Being-with in terms of our "anybody" selves. These public possessions as common encounterables may be presupposed as the human nature of Dasein, its very own-ness. Such public "ownness," when understood as how we are with others in a state of Care, is Dasein's Being-with. This state of Being-with does not usually require explanation, because the common sense world of the "anybody" is so presupposed in the non-reflective public state that it requires the agency of philosophy to make us aware of how it exists. On this point Heidegger went to the length of demonstrating to the common sense world what the absence of the "anybody" frame of reference would involve.[12]

In his thinking upon the "I-myself" Heidegger also wanted to transcend the teachings of his teacher Edmund Husserl by founding our way of Being-in-a-world not in a transcendental subject, or a private, separable self, but in terms of the public commonality of the "anybody." In sum, our existence in a world reveals a primordial relation to an implied sociality that he called "Being-with." This is the existential condition of common, public expectations, the common ground of our sociality. This Being-with refers to the common competence of Dasein to be with others understandingly in Solicitude (*Fürsorge*). Our Being, in short, is a Being-with-others, and we are with others through the a priori capacity to make a commonality possible. To be with others is an own-most possibility of ourselves.

Our understanding of Being-with in terms of our common sociality is the positive sense for Heidegger of how we are commonly in a world. Being-with is of positive significance, for it is necessitated of Dasein that it possess a public, conforming, and social dimension. We have, in other words, a commonality in our "I-myself" which requires for its Being-in-the-world an expected and normal way of referring to and dealing with others. In this sense the "I-myself" exists, in significant part, in its conformity to the "one" or "anybody" or "they," and it shares or refers to a commonality of significance. However, Heidegger alluded to two aspects of unease or struggle within the positive sense of *das Man*. One is what Heidegger termed Distantiality (*Abständigkeit*), which represents the fact that as Dasein must seek in its everyday sense to approximate the public, positive sense of the "anybody," it hesitates to roam too far from public use and expectation. As Dasein attempts to remain normally viable in the public "one," it must differentiate and adjust to its circumstances, either consciously or subconsciously; it must relate to the varying assumptions of whatever public milieu it is in, be it home or workplace, religious or political gathering, etc.; it must "distance" itself from one set of public expectations as it adjusts to a different context; it must relate separately to varying contexts. This continual process of adjustment is a struggle which is nevertheless possible, because our anonymous primordial "withness" assumes a public possibility for itself without question. Dasein is a repository of average public intelligibility and shared expectations and perspectives, in our Being-with others. The "I-myself" floats upon a sea of assumptions about how it is with others in a world. This assumed and pre-interpreted manner in which we are with others is a central and positive fact about the way Dasein is in the world. It is the condition of Dasein that makes society, custom, common usage, and institutional behavior possible.

However, a second type of unease exists within our "anybody" self, because our Being-with, our public commonality, is largely forgotten and covered up by Dasein. Dasein continues to think of itself as a transparent ego, a *solus ipse* present-to-hand. Existence seems to Dasein to be the univocal particularity of this ego. Dasein forgets that it is a multiplicity of roles which are socially predefined, and its possibilities are largely socially prescribed. Dasein forgets how little its existence is removed from its public significance in the everydayness of the "anybody"; it forgets that even what Heidegger defined as authentic existence is but a modification of our public sociality. Despite this self-confident delusion of the ego, Heidegger positively asserted that the "who of Dasein" is primarily defined by reference to this "anybody" self.

But there is another sense of Dasein's publicness which must now come to the center of our study, the defective or inauthentic aspect of our otherwise useful and necessary public "I-myself." This is our Being-with *in extremis.* For while we are public in our everydayness, in the positive sense, the self may be so lost or submerged in its public self that it cannot or will not actualize or identify those possibilities that it possesses as its authentic ownness. Not only may it relinquish its freedom to the other, it may be so fallen into the state of the "anybody" or "one" that it does not identify to itself the means of its distraction or emancipation. It becomes captivated in its actualities. For Heidegger this captivated *das Man* Existential plays a central but defective role among our possibilities. *Das Man* in this negative sense is the German equivalent of the following English linguistic uses: "Everyone does that" or "Nobody thinks that way anymore" or "What are they saying?" It is here an implied person or group which is also an abstraction, but an abstraction of the self's possibilities that is merely prohibitive or normative without reason or alternative possibility.

The term *das Man* was Heidegger's way of expressing both the authentic and defective senses of this *das Man* Existential, which is an a priori part of our Being-with in the world. The authentic "who of Dasein" is not a rare or abnormal self which is apart from all that is social; rather, Being-one's-self is a modification of the public self.[13] The authentic sense of the "anybody" is seen as the source from which the "who of Dasein" is constructed. But the negative sense of the "anybody" occurs when our legitimate public self falls into "leveling" or the constrictive pattern distinguished above. Here is *das Man* in the sense of Kierkegaard's crowd. As in the thinking of Kierkegaard before him, Heidegger noted that it is when our public self forces the suppression of all differences and imposes conformity as our only possibility that the public self translates into the defective aspect of *das Man*. Here *das Man* is not only public but appears as the only possibility of our existence. In other words, it is when the defective sense of the public appears as a total necessity of the self that *das Man* is negative.[14]

If we step out of *das Man* by taking hold of ourselves, we seem to put ourselves into a questionable or abnormal position. It seems easier to accept or "go along with" the present actuality until the next one comes along. Yet our dilemma is more complicated than this, because Dasein itself tends to perform a covering operation in which it slides into the norms of *das Man*, and hides from itself alternative possibilities. Dasein here remains in bondage to an "anybody" who grants it permission or approval. The "anybody" claims an obvious legitimacy that demands an obvious conformity. Such a situation frequently occurs in a political setting, such as one observed recently on a university campus during a visit of a presidential candidate: in order to force a unified and chanting mass at his university address, the candidate's "men" would allow no students at this public university to carry signs supporting his opponent; no other possibilities but this one candidate's would be tolerated or accepted in the group. But such *das Man* requirements were supported in turn by university officials as apparently legitimate, and students accepted this stricture as "normal" or "legitimized" by the mass and power of the situation. *Das Man* is here the mentality of exclusion or inclusion upon one criterion, often ideological or political. The "they" or "one" becomes the agent in Dasein's "who" that obscures the free possibilities of either an individual or a group. In this sense *das Man* is in untruth because it deflects or obscures our own-most possibilities of being other than the "one." This being in the untruth of actuality by covering-up is for Heidegger the inauthentic or defective sense of our Being-with. The behavior of the "anybody" is here confined to the fact not that it must be with others in the common sociality of meanings and expectations, but that it must cover up and obscure the truth that it has the possibility of being other than it is.

It was Heidegger's contention that the manner in which we lose ourselves in the other is in fact a part of ourselves. Being-with-others in the world *and* the "they-self" are Existentials of Dasein itself. In this sense we cannot do without them or be apart from them. In the negative condition of *das Man* we may be the "owners" of the kind of sociality of Dasein which is exclusively outside of ourselves, and in a defective condition; this means that Dasein can attempt to become present to itself and to others in the mode of inauthenticity. But Heidegger's self-imposed task was one of describing and understanding the self as *das Man*, whether it be the authentic or inauthentic self of Dasein.[15]

Nevertheless, while Heidegger did not attempt to advance moral claims or subjective priorities about *das Man*, his description of defective Dasein does appear to possess a moral significance. We see, for example, that when Dasein is so appropriated into the external public self that it "loses sight of itself," it becomes dominated by norms that may be questioned by an ordinary moral sense; it becomes transformed into an identity which does not seem to be its very own, but is assumed for the time. Half-knowingly and half-indeliberately, Dasein turns itself over to an average expectancy and everydayness which may obscure its possibilities and its history through the tranquilizations of a crowd. This crowd does not require expectancies or possibility; it acts as dictator. In his *Walden* Henry David Thoreau spoke of a clothing clerk who pointed to an article of Thoreau's clothing and said, "They are not wearing that anymore." Here *das Man* was tempting Thoreau to assign his self-estimate in dress to the vague yet demanding norm of a fashionable "they." He must do what "they" do, dress as "they" dress, judge as "they" judge. Dasein was dissolved in the *das Man* status into the possibilities of the other. Yet in this condition the other tends to vanish into inconspicuousness. It is here that the real dictatorship of *das Man* is revealed. In our seeing and judging as "they" see and judge, taking pleasure in what they take pleasure in, *das Man* becomes more hidden and inconspicuous. Through our constant reference to it, or assumption of it, *das Man* becomes less definite and dissolves into Dasein's everydayness.[16] In this defective state Dasein turns itself over to the impersonal yet authoritative "they," and this agency tends to become our own-most possibility. The "they" will seek to appear as the very foundation of the self, and to possess a meaning or normative content which is passed off as obvious. The "they" acts as a higher intelligibility and authority, and it hides in the everydayness of Dasein. When the "who" of Dasein becomes the "anybody," then Dasein in its everydayness has leveled its possibilities to averageness. As the triumph of averageness, inauthentic Dasein seeks "liberation" in the "anybody"; it seeks unconsciously to accept the public way in which the self and the world get interpreted.[17] Dasein here becomes a concerned absorption in the world. In this state the "I-myself," and any legitimacy it may possess, never surpasses the "anybody."

While the condition we are describing may seem dramatically negative, and while it may seem that we should do everything in our power to disengage from the "they," Heidegger tells us that we are given to ourselves most proximally as the "anybody" and remain so for the most part.[18] At this point it would seem that such a conclusion nullifies any possibility of a self that is its very own-ness, that yet belongs to itself in the massification of everyday life. There is such a self, what we shall call the "authentic self," and the paths to it, which always lie open to us, we shall soon discover. But first we must observe how Heidegger, in Sections 35 to 38 of *Being and Time*, continued to unpack through his phenomenological description the status of *das Man* by elucidating the Falling (*Verfallen*) of Dasein. This description utilized the following elements: Idle Talk (*Gerede*), Curiosity (*Neugier*), and Ambiguity (*Zweideutigkeit*). All of these elements bear a crucial relation to *das Man* and hence must now be examined.

Through Idle Talk Dasein falls into an everyday interpretation of the world in a specific use of language. Here Dasein attempts to hide its possibilities from itself by assigning them over to a kind of slanted linguistic determination. In Idle Talk Dasein uses such expressions as "They say the university can't survive financially without collegiate sports," or "Everyone knows that minorities are anti-Republican." In such covering statements there is no commitment to the truth or concern for it. Such expressions are a way of preventing an honest search for what is real, while at the same time asserting some definiteness.

The everyday speech of the "they," Idle Talk, is generated by the second element of fallenness, Curiosity. Here Dasein seems to come to a definite state through its apparent concern for something as a spectator. But at the same time it remains in a state of concealed indifference; it seems observational yet is neutral in its relation to the world. In its search for distraction and novelty, it is blind to the actuality in front of it. For example, it will ask, "How are you?" but in a covertly indifferent way; or "Who was killed?" without intending any particular significance. In this manner Dasein avoids authentic concern for the world.

The third mode of fallen Dasein Heidegger terms Ambiguity. In its search for tranquillity and averageness, Dasein here sees the world as theory and abstraction, while remaining neutral

and passive. The demands of Care and of sociohistorical actualities are dissolved into theoretical indifference, such as a population theorist looking at starvation in Africa in terms of statistical averages, or a psychologist taking a clinical posture while
probing a patient's psychic suffering, pretending in his/her role
as a doctor or counselor that he or she doesn't have the same
human anxieties as the patient. Dasein here seeks to lie in a
manufactured indifference or theoreticality. In this attitude the
world and its Cares have "already been thought about," and
other possible interpretations of the significances (the starvation or suffering)—interpretations that might be personal, spiritual, poetic, etc.—are closed off as unimportant.

These three modes provide a sort of grounding for the "they"
or the negative side of *das Man*. In these states Dasein seeks to
become a sort of "nobody" through its surrender to the
"they."[19] Dasein's natural Being-with status "gives way" to these
inauthentic modes in the sense that it loses its awareness of
itself in its concern with everyday dealings. Through its forgetfulness of its own-most Being and its possibilities it becomes
inauthentic (*uneigentlich*) or fallen. Fallenness in this context is
defined as our inauthentic identification with the other who is
guided by idle talk, curiosity and ambiguity.[20] All of these states
are components of falling which the crowd tends to see as the
normal, standard, acceptable accommodation to obviousness.
In our desire to flee anxiety, choice, and responsibility, we find
it convenient to slide into this state of fall. Fallen into a world
of averageness, we are part of the "they," in which we avoid the
possible through interpretations which are ready-made by the
other. We are in Kierkegaard's world of leveling and publicness. Dasein has so fallen out of itself that it restricts its possibilities to the "they" exclusively; in this state the whole of our
Being-with status seems more or less exhausted in *das Man*.[21]
Dasein seeks to become a totality as depersonalization, and in
its fall it seeks tranquilization and distraction through the con-
cealments of worldliness. It would repress from itself the possibilities of its being otherwise.

After his discussion of fallenness, with its actualities of idle
talk, curiosity, and ambiguity, Heidegger continued his analysis
of everyday Dasein in Division Two, Chapter II, Sections 54 to

60 under the general title "Dasein's Attestation of an Authentic Potentiality-for-Being, and Resoluteness." In these sections Heidegger was attempting to show not only that we may lose ourselves in our everyday Being-with, but that Dasein is able to extract itself from its immersion in *das Man*. While the dominant tendency of everyday Dasein is to level or dim its "I-myself" to the vague averageness (*Durchschnittlichkeit*) of the "they" or "anybody," it is also important to remember that Dasein is never a total incorporation into the "one." The "I-myself" retains in part not only its own possibility of self-retrieval but also the responsibility of retrieving its own-ness from *das Man*. The first means of retrieval is what Heidegger designated as resoluteness (*Entschlossenheit*). It is through resoluteness that Dasein calls itself from the "they." It is through Dasein's resolve to be itself, to belong to itself alone, that Dasein retrieves itself from the "anybody." Dasein may ignore the call to be itself, or may hide from it in the distractions of the "they," but Dasein remains always open to its possibilities, its truth, in resolution. Even in the state of fallenness Dasein may still take hold of itself, by distinguishing itself from its lostness in actualities and regaining its freedom, its I-myself-ness. In the defective *das Man* pole, the qualities of everydayness gain a mastery over the self; in the authentic and resolute state, this everydayness of self-concealment is recognized and Dasein seeks to be open to itself as possibility. In this manner Dasein's authentic potential for Being and resoluteness are closely linked. For Heidegger our authentic Being-with is grounded in the possible, while our inauthentic Being-with is grounded in actualities which we assume to be unchanging. For example, in Idle Talk Dasein assumes the unchangeable truth of "They say X." This is the actuality of fallenness, which demands that judgments and events could never be other than what the crowd says. On the other hand, our authentic Being-with is open and able to make its own interpretations and determinations, through resoluteness. Possibility is one of Dasein's primordial constituents; it is our own-most able-to-be-ness (*Seinkönnen*), and we live by the projection of our possibilities into the world. This means that the world does not exist for us indifferently but in terms of our

projections of possibilities. For Heidegger the agency of human freedom in resoluteness is established in our possessing possibilities, and freedom can never be understood or even described apart from Dasein's awareness of its possibility of Being in the world in definite ways.

When that existential significance of possibility gets hidden from Dasein, so that Dasein falls short of its possibilities or hides from them or dissolves them in the possibilities of the crowd, then there is a second means for the human being to rise from its deficient condition to authentic status: in addition to resoluteness, Dasein must be open in its Being to the voice of conscience (*Gewissen*). Heidegger indicated by this Existential the condition in which Dasein refuses to live in forfeiture to the defective states of the Fall, and is called out of them. Conscience is the calling of Dasein to itself, from its distraction or self-forgetfulness to its affirmation and responsibility to be itself. The presence of conscience was Heidegger's way of indicating that Dasein exists in a state of incompletion to itself. It is always in debt, always "short of" the states it resolves to be, or ought to be. In this sense of incompletion Dasein is always guilty (*Schüld*). But this guilt is not to be understood in the traditional sense of sin, but as an Existential of Dasein. Conscience is that which recognizes guilt. Conscience and guilt are the clearest and deepest indication of the nature of the self. They are both elements that compose our very own-ness, and they make possible the state of moral blameworthiness. Because Dasein is capable of being in such a deficient condition of blameworthiness, it is also capable of calling itself from it, and this it does. The "who of Dasein" in its very Care calls itself to its own possibilities. It usually happens that Dasein has released itself into some *das Man* identity with a crowd and with presuppositions which are covers for its fallenness; but in such a situation Dasein's call of conscience will seek to retrieve it from such participation and return itself to those possibilities which are its own.

Both guilt and conscience are grounded in the fact that even in its possibilities Dasein remains always lacking, always falling short, a finite Being which can never possess an absolute or eternal status. It can never give to itself a final definition through either its creations or its projects. Therefore, Dasein must be resolved to the fact that it is at once its own possibilities *and* a falling short of them. This condition creates in Dasein an anxiety over its own imperfections and finitude—and this very anxiety provides a third means, beyond resolution and conscience-with-guilt, for authenticity and retrieval of the self from the nullification by the crowd. For anxiety brings Dasein to an awareness of itself through its very fallings and finitude; anxiety forces us to look at what we have and have not become; it recognizes that we have potential for Being, and not simply the being of the crowd.[22] In anxiety and guilt, through resoluteness and conscience, Dasein appropriates its freedom to become its authentic own-ness; its bondage to the crowd is released through its disclosure of its finite possibilities. In the call of conscience, guilt, and anxiety it resolutely creates a life that belongs to itself and not to the "they." Released from the distractions of the "they," it becomes a freedom toward its own death.

A fourth means to resolute and authentic existence is Dasein's utilization of its heritage and community. Heidegger affirmed that authentic possibility can never be separated from these.[23] It is out of our past associations and traditions that we create our own future. Michael Zimmerman has developed Heidegger's thesis that one of the reasons we of contemporary times are so alienated from our authentic selves is our removal from our roots of heritage and community to an alien, anonymous, urbanized, and technological mass-society. We now accept our possibilities largely in terms of economic satisfactions, the stockpiling of material reserves, and the exploitation of nature to this end.[24] So totalizing is the modern mass that Heidegger seemed to imply that our authenticity urges us to flee urbanization, just as he, for example, removed himself to the mountains.

While there is a positive function for our social existence, Heidegger's *das Man* was meant to remind us that through our participation in the mass we can become almost incapable of either self-direction or independent evaluation. It is the role of the "I-myself" as an authentic self to resist such a tendency—the tendency to cover up its capacity, to nullify its significance, to flee its possibilities, to lose sight of itself in its dealings with the world. Against this tendency to blindness, it is the task of resolute Dasein to work out of the "they" and find the existence it can take hold of as its own. Many Heidegger scholars have noticed two final means by which Dasein removes itself from untruth and the dictates of the "they." One of these is that resolute Dasein discloses its authentic nature to the fullest when it comes to the recognition that it is itself the "Clearing for Being." Authentic Dasein, in other words, is an openness not only to its own Being but also, more fundamentally, to Being itself. Here Dasein becomes the "Clearing" for truth and freedom to its possibilities. Dasein is no longer content to rest in its everydayness, and it ceases to draw its interpretation of itself from the "they." Not only does the "they" here become more visible, but it is seen as that part of Dasein's nature which is no longer allowed the dominance it usually enjoys.

The other of these final means is the recognition of death. It is in the realization of death as its own-most possibility that Dasein comes to the awareness that it cannot conceive of itself in public possibilities alone. In death is the possibility of not having any possibilities. Also in the realization that it is going to die, Dasein comes to see that it is thrown into a worldly condition that was determined neither by its choices nor by the crowd into which it has tried to lose itself. Its possibilities of public socialization as *das Man* are always outstripped by the final possibility of death. Because of finitude, anxiety, and death, the great sources of Dasein's insight into its Being-in-the-world, Dasein cannot simply tranquilize itself by a flight into *das Man*. The awareness of death, then, can be a positive source of our consideration of how we are in the world; it can be an element of our freedom and resoluteness. In this sense Spinoza's dictum that the wise man thinks of nothing less than death is false. The reality of death serves to save Dasein from enticement into the untruth of the "they."

(D) The "Anybody" as Historical Agent

We have seen in summary of our thesis so far that Dasein's Being-in-the-world does not make of it a solitary or subjective "I-myself." Our Being-in-the-world is from beginning to end a primordial Being-with-others. This fact is indicated by the existential term *Mitsein*. We are in the world as co-existence in a partly-positive relationship of solicitude and inter-subjectivity. Our Being-with-others-in-a-world is a crucial element of our authentic makeup. In Section C we followed Heidegger's analysis of how it is possible to be with others in a defective and conforming state which surrenders to actuality and fallenness. This self-repressing state is the negative side of what Heidegger called *das Man*. Here the self falls into a world of anonymous sociality in idle talk, curiosity, and ambiguity. The "I-myself" is not only hidden by its participation in the "anybody" of *das Man*, but it participates in a mass self which drifts in depersonal existence. A public self covers the "I-myself" and tends to nullify resolute Dasein's attempt to take hold of itself. This is the defective or negative sense of our Being-with others.

But for this section of Chapter III we must return to the positive role of our Being-with others in the world, in order to explore further how it possesses a positive significance for our social functioning, in particular our historical Being. Put another way, our Being-with in society and history refers to our common public nature in time. Being-with has both a social and historical dimension. In this section we shall see that our Being-with has an important but virtually ignored relation to the Historicality of man. The historical sense of our Being-with in Heidegger's thought seems to have been drawn from the influence of Wilhelm Dilthey (1833-1911). We must now briefly examine this influence.

For Dilthey human life possesses a unique way of being in time which he designated as Historicality. The Historicality of life indicates that human Beings possess the form and the materials of intelligible intersubjective existence through history. Human life understands itself as an existence in time which is understandable, because both the historical actor and the historical interpreter possess a common nature. The nature of those who make history and culture is a common possession of those who understand it. For Dilthey, the human studies (*Geisteswissenschaften*) have never adequately understood their grounding in Historicality, and it was Dilthey's greatness to have shown that as radically historical Beings, we (and our works) cannot be understood apart from the Historicality of our existence.

Historicality refers to the fact that when we examine our lived experience, we find it is a unity in which the past is retained in memory in the lived present, and the future is anticipated from out of our present. Our experience is a constant advance upon itself in which the present becomes the past and the future becomes the present. Because the anticipated possibility of future experience is integrated with past and present, Dilthey wanted to show that human life in history is not a finally constituted or fixed existence as is that of a stone. Nor is its temporality determined by correlation to clock time. Human life and its world are experienced as flux, as an intermingling of past, present and future.

In this flux there also exists a mutually referential status between human life and its social and historical environment. The historical and human studies are made possible through the shared existence of those who make history and society and those who understand it. We are in principle historical Beings who are in the world inter-subjectively with others like us. For Dilthey it is through the method of understanding (*Verstehen*) that the disciplined interpretation of the experience of the other (through its outward expressions in actions, creation, or symbols) is made possible. Such expressions Dilthey called life assertions (*Lebensäusserungen*). *Verstehen* becomes here the attempt of the interpreter to derive from these expressions the meanings, values, and purposes that were intended by their creator. The implication of this is that human Beings live in a sociohistorical world of shared intelligibility. The significance of human life is inseparable from the fact that the individual does not exist apart from his/her relationship to others in historical time. The significance of our human Being arises, for Dilthey, in the sociohistorical domain of the public, and Heidegger's attempt to give priority to the human Being's sociality and historicality was a derivation from Dilthey. The "anybody" or *das Man* as history is a legacy from Dilthey, and it is to this element in Heidegger that we must now turn.

For Heidegger, as for Dilthey, Dasein's existence is only comprehensible in the context of Historicality. For us to understand Heidegger's Historicality it is necessary to provide a phenomenological description of how Dasein happens in time. This occurs in Chapters V and VI, Sections 72-83. First, the "who of Dasein" exists as a stretching (*Strecke*) from its past to its future, up to the point of death. Such a "stretching" he calls the historizing (*Geschehen*) of Dasein. It is in historizing, Dasein's Being in time, that the "who of Dasein" is revealed, for Dasein's "who" can never be separated from its Historicality.[25] Dasein is the unity of how it stretches or happens in time, and this unity is composed of the elements of Heritage, Fate, and Destiny. We must briefly examine these elements in order to see the relationship of Historicality to the "anybody."

Heritage (*Erbschaft*) refers to Dasein's having been in the past. It is the aggregate of those past states which compose its present actuality. Dasein must accept those actions, creations, and choices of its past as its own-ness. These actions, creations, and choices can be handed down to the future as the prior states of itself. These having-been states then become in turn possibilities for future repetition (*Wiederholen*), models that act as possibilities for imitation for future human Being. It is the possibility of such retrieval of past existence that makes historical science possible at all.

Fate (*Schicksal*) is the second element of Dasein's Historicality, and it refers to the possibilities to which Dasein orients itself through resolute choice. These choices are fateful in their historical significance, and it is only such choices that release us from indecisiveness and conformity to *das Man*. In its fatefulness, Dasein is aware of its limited possibilities and at the same time of its having created them. The irresolute mass (*das Man*) can have no such fate, and consequently no authentic Historicality. The resolute Being listens to the call of conscience away from external routine; and because such Dasein is self-directive and creative, it is the author of its own fate. Irresolute Dasein does not choose or create its authentic possibilities, but floats indecisively from possibility to possibility.[26] In contrast to this tendency, fateful Dasein appropriates its possibilities even in the face of its fallenness and finitude.

Destiny (*Geschick*) is the third component of Dasein's Historicality, and it refers to Dasein's authentic relation to groups, peoples, and nations. This relation is grounded in Dasein's Being-with Existential. Such a Being-with-as-Destiny may be either authentic or inauthentic. An authentic destiny will possess a resolute and self-defining characteristic. Here a group or people will reject the irresolute and distracted behavior of merely *das Man* collectives. Only resolute peoples can appropriate the destiny of an era, for authentic Dasein is only revealed in the Historicality of self-determination.

On the other hand, both the authentic and inauthentic modes of historical existence must be distinguished if the full significance of this historical process is to be revealed. To this end Heidegger told us that we must examine inauthentic Historicality.[27] He noted that while Dasein historizes with others in a common destiny, this Being-with status becomes defective when Dasein forgets itself in *das Man*. In such a state Dasein becomes blind to its possibilities, avoids decisions that its peers avoid, and loses itself in waiting and forgetting. Seeing its existence and that of others as a mere succession of moments, the individual falls into a passive state without any moment of vision for the possibilities of the self or group. The habits, ignorance, and vaguenesses of *das Man* disperse Dasein into states of non-accountability for the future and the past. Any chance of forming a unity of heritage, fate, or destiny into a program of action is lost. The "now" of present-at-hand desires or diversions nullifies any sense of greater purpose, and the prefabricated expectations of defective *das Man* disperse any sense of heritage, fate, or destiny.[28] This defective manner of Being in historical time is the inauthentic Historicality of *das Man*.

When mass behavior replaces resolute and authentic Dasein as the subject-matter of history, explanatory methods and materials are often brought in by social scientists to explain the regularities of *das Man*. For this reason any Diltheyan thematizing of Dasein's Historicality by reference to social systems, methodological subjects, historicism, or the critique of historical reason became for Heidegger inauthentic historiography. Heidegger confined authentic historical studies to the revelations of Dasein's authentic possibilities. Heidegger's position, in fact, tended to bifurcate history into authentic and inauthentic dimensions. When defective or fallen, *das Man* tended for him to become a sort of sub-historical entity with a life below that of authentic Historicality. This tendency is better understood, I believe, if we remember that Heidegger's thought on this matter was a residue not of Dilthey's, in this case, but of Kierkegaard's position in the *Postscript* which postulated that only the actions of authentic individuality are constitutive either of historical science or a universal history.[29] We must now look at the thought of Friedrich Nietzsche, in light of Heidegger's appropriation of his insights into mass nihilism; we will relate Nietzsche to the themes we have developed in Heidegger, and then examine Heidegger's response to Nietzsche.

Chapter Four

Nietzsche, Nihilism and the Herd

(A) Nietzsche's Assumptions

No examination of the existential critique of *das Man* can be complete without reference to the thought of Friedrich Nietzsche (1844-1900). Heidegger's reflections upon *das Man* and its nihilism are in part a response to his confrontation with both Nietzsche and contemporary technology. Heidegger was among the first to recognize that Nietzsche cannot be understood in terms of the all-too-general conception of him as an irresponsible thinker who had no serious philosophical dimensions. Instead, Heidegger's studies and ponderings led him to the conclusion that Nietzsche was one of the few who foresaw the demoralizing human and philosophical conditions of the twentieth century. In order to grasp Nietzsche's influence upon Heidegger and better understand Nietzsche's thinking upon the mass, it is necessary to address his thought in a preliminary and general manner, then to focus specifically upon his thesis of the relation between the mass and nihilism. We shall then address Heidegger's incorporation of these Nietzschean elements into his own thought. We may begin with some general biographical facts of Nietzsche's life, then move to his central philosophical assumptions, at which point we shall be in a better position to understand his relation to Heidegger's theses on the masses, technology, and nihilism.[1]

Friedrich Nietzsche was born in Prussian Saxony in 1844, into a family with several generations of ministers. A gifted student, he received a classical education at the Gymnasium at Pforta. At first the young Nietzsche was a devout Christian, but he soon changed to a posture of militant atheism. Arthur Schopenhauer (1788-1860) became the greatest intellectual influence on his young life. Schopenhauer had held that the world is, in its innermost parts, a blind force of will that appears as craving and force in human life. This will is in constant strife with the resistances of other wills, so that the result for the individual is frustration and incompletion. It is the proper office of philosophy, art, and religion to understand the will and to show the real basis of pessimism, i.e., the doctrine that the sum total of evil in the universe outweighs the sum total of good. Schopenhauer's position was developed in *The World as Will and Representation* (1818). Nietzsche would later accept Schopenhauer's doctrine of the centrality of the will in his own philosophy, but he would reject Schopenhauer's pessimism in his own philosophy of the will to power.

Nietzsche later studied classical philology at the Universities of Bonn and Leipzig, and he was subsequently appointed to the chair of classical philology at the University of Basel in 1869. He became a friend of Richard Wagner (1813-1883) and his wife Cosima, but he later rejected both Wagner and his doctrines because of what he considered their decadence and incipient Christian apologetics. Within ten years of his Basel appointment he also rejected the whole university connection. But retirement brought no relief, because of continuing health problems. While visiting health resorts he wrote his major books, including his unfinished *The Will to Power*. Alone, unrecognized, and in ill health, he spent his last years plagued with alienation and suffering; in fact, he was diagnosed as insane for the last eleven years of his life. While largely unrecognized in his lifetime, he became world famous soon after his death in 1900.

At the closing of the nineteenth century Nietzsche announced to an optimistic and self-satisfied era his understanding of the implications of the coming of nihilism. This term indicated for him a disbelief in the existence of God, truth, and final reality. It also indicated the devolution of higher values into equality of all values and into the invalid praise of progress, of objective truth or value, and of the unquestioned philosophical assumptions of natural science. From the beginning of his thinking life Nietzsche had confronted the fact of nihilism and he now stood openly opposed to the major ingredients of modernism: the decline of the feudal order, the rise of the national state, democracy, liberalism, and industrialism. He also remained hostile to European and especially German imperialism. He believed that the new urbanization with its population expansion had derailed traditional *Gemeinschaft* social allegiances and traditional loyalties. He predicted that the rise of a unified German empire under Bismarck (1815-1898) would be the beginning of the wars and cultural philistinism that would come to dominate Europe. He thought that because Germany had rejected the humanism of both Goethe and classical philosophical idealism, Germany had become the enemy of the classical heritage of Greece and Rome. In fact, since the Reformation Germany was creating as the model of Europe a mass society that was both democratic and socialistic. The result was a generally leveling influence of the masses in Western Europe, and subsequently the Western World. Like Kierkegaard before him, Nietzsche understood his mission to be one of cultural, spiritual, and moral criticism of a nihilistic modern era. Through his thinking and writing he attempted to make the modern era aware of its own plight; he attempted to smash the false idols of his age.

Nevertheless, the assumptions and methods of Nietzsche are not easily stated or understood. Contrary to popular opinion, he is one of the most difficult of all philosophers. His thought is not systematic, and his conclusions often take the form of thought-experiments which will later be formulated from different perspectives. But at least the following theses are representative of the mature Nietzsche. The world, he thought, possesses no thing-in-itself after the doctrines of Kant, and reason cannot reveal an independently existing world. There are no ultimately real facts, truths, or realities; there are only interpretations of the world. Nietzsche's thought here is the thesis of "perspectivism," i.e., that we do not transcend the personal perspectives through which the world is given to us. Perspectives are always finite in their representations of reality, and they always omit the remainder of the world which they do not reveal. In this sense perspectives always involve a certain falsification of the world, yet all knowing must be founded in the limits of perspective. There are no perspectiveless facts or theo-

ries, because the human observer must project upon phenomena a sense or meaning that is itself coherent within a point of
view, and all knowledge and science depend upon a prior
interpretive perspective.[2] Conceptualization can only confine
the dynamic flow of experience into linguistic and conceptual
forms which we may mistake for the world itself. Yet for Nietzsche the perspectives of the world must be so simplified and
thematized that our interpretations may sustain human life.

Nietzsche's doctrine of voluntarism holds that reason is the
servant of the instincts, especially the will. The engine of
human behavior is not intellect, reason, or knowledge, but the
striving to dominate and create the world in which we exist.
Nietzsche designated this striving the will to power, especially as
it expresses itself as self-determination. This will to power is the
innermost force in human life and the universe at large. "The
world is the will to power, and nothing more, and you are the
will to power and nothing more."[3] Our living is will to power
when it is directed to resistance, destruction, and force necessary to life. It is the striving to dominate other wills to its purposes. In the lower biological organisms this power is dominantly the struggle to survive. In human beings it may take the
form of striving to knowledge and truth, for these are also
means of creating and dominating the world.[4]

The human individual, then, like all else, is a manifestation of
the will to power, and the most authentic expression of this will
in the individual is the strength that accepts its own fate (*amor
fati*). It is from this "love of fate" that Nietzsche rejected
Schopenhauer's pessimism. The will to power is not evil, nor
should it be rejected. Evil cannot be avoided through the denial
or destruction of the will, and such negations are only the way
of the weak. The strong individuals will accept their fate, and
they will have the strength to affirm their lives in spite of their
struggle, terror, and final tragedy. We must expend the power
to create the illusions, dreams, and interpretations which mask
the terror of existence in nature. Part of this masking is the
attempt to humanize the universe through the creations of art,
religion, and philosophy. But such creations can allow the weak
to take refuge from the world as it actually is. The strong
understand these creations to be the maskings that they are, but

the weak refuse to see beyond these and seek to substitute an imaginary world for existence as it is. Their masking perspectives become the essence of a real or "higher" world. The world as it is then becomes for them the "negative universe," a place of terror, power, and fate. Reality is perceived by the weak in the imaginary perspective of an ideal sphere such as that created by Plato and later by Christianity. But the strong never substitute dreams for reality, nor do they demand that their dreams and creations must be accepted as the only conditions upon which human life can be affirmed. According to Nietzsche, even culture itself has come to pose as a higher reality than nature, and the weak suppose that culture is over against nature and the only authentic condition for life itself. But nature itself provides deeper, more convincing norms and actualities for contemporary humanity. The strong do not need to sanctify the conventions of society as the ground of their values, but they instead realize themselves through creativity and the will to power.

For Nietzsche the greatness of the Greeks lay in their power and courage to accept existence as it is, and in their affirmation of the human condition with all its chance, danger, and tragedy. This strength and affirmation is the real greatness of the Greeks, a greatness which is especially evident in their drama. In this art they were able to affirm reality without masking it or perishing before it. In their drama they turned the tragic sense of life into the ideal beauty of the Apollonian life-form of measure and light. Yet they were able to preserve in their drama the suffering, sensate, and tragic will of the god Dionysius. Through their synthesis of these two forms, the Apollonian and the Dionysian, they gave formal expression to the affirmative aspects of life. But for Nietzsche it was the intent of Socratic rationalism to undermine this synthetic achievement. It was the mission of Socrates to repress and destroy the entire Dionysian element in existence and to promote only the Apollonian forms of reason, knowledge, and restraint. Socratic rationalism led to the destruction of tragedy, which is significantly the artistic expression of the Dionysian elements of existence. Socrates would pretend that the will to power was negated through his creation of a "higher world" exemplified in the Apollonian idealizations of life. Here began the bifurcation of the Western tradition into the forces of anti-life and those of the life-affirming will to power.

The strong have always tended to impute the conditions of power to the world, and it is only in this way that they will consent to humanize the universe. The strong will not substitute Socratic idealism for the Dionysian projection of will, power, suffering, and passion. They will not understand the world in the moral terms of Socrates or Jesus. The "single" life-affirming ones must resurrect Dionysius and join him to the Apollonian god for the creation of a new being who can join realism and ideality in a new affirmation of life. This is for Nietzsche the authentic birth of tragedy.

For Nietzsche traditional Western philosophy is not only sick but dead. It has died of a moral and emotional illness which needs curing in our era, an illness whose onset came with the Enlightenment's worship of reason and objectivity at the expense of subjective existence. A new thinking must come to the aid of our contemporary nihilistic situation and interpret a world which demands our decisions about both its meaning and value. This thinking must be able to face and command the plethora of man's perspectives through a new experimentalism with respect to the questions of human life. We must judge both thinking and valuation by the following criterion: Do these enhance or diminish human life? Human life must become an experiment. But its conclusions will not be considered mirrors of eternal truth; rather, they will provide a "joyful wisdom" with respect to the dangers and demands of human life. That wisdom which enhances the scope and power of life is the end to be sought. This joyful wisdom will discount any "higher" metaphysical reality as useless for our condition, the result of weakness and will-less-ness. The previous metaphysical and religious world pictures which provided security and comfort are no longer viable in our time.

Put briefly, in Nietzsche's world God is dead, and this means that the divine world of eternal value and salvation is no longer relevant to our condition. The existence of God as an absolute subject who provides transcendent truth and value to man is no longer a useful interpretation of the world. Yet the residue of such a creature still lingers in contemporary life. God's death is a historical and psychological event that is evident to some, yet the masses, which Nietzsche designated as the herd, do not realize this event fully, nor do they understand its implications. In a word, the herd masks the arrival of nihilism, yet it lives out its themes. The masses do not understand that God is no longer a positive presence in human life. This sense, rather than the fact that a divine creature has actually died, is the meaning of the phrase "God is dead." The concept of God no longer allows for a viable interpretation of existence, but persists as a failed experiment that must be abandoned. Nietzsche's problematic was not to disprove the existence of God, but to show to our era the moral and intellectual implications of the death of God in our lives.

A clue to understanding these implications is to be found in his analysis of the genealogy of morals. In Nietzsche's meta-ethical attempt to describe the phenomenon of morals he spoke of the will to power as manifest historically in the forms of the master and the slave. In all master morality, he told us, the will to power is accepted for what it is. In the case of slave morality, the attempt is to hide the reality of power from others, but to use it for a secret advantage. Both forms of moral life have developed from definite historical conditions which Nietzsche attempted to reveal. The most important of these conditions were the Judeo-Roman and the Christian-Roman historical traditions. Both the Jewish and Christian traditions represented for Nietzsche the slave moralities of the weak, in the grip of their Roman masters. In these traditions the "weak" assumed a lowly, selfless posture, but at the same time attempted to impose the value of submission on the strong. They envisioned a God who evaluated the will, egoism, and dominance of the strong as sins which could only be remitted through submission to the tenets of the Judeo-Christian tradition. Here the weak utilized their own disqualifications as means to obtain reconciliation with God and power over their masters. But this exercise of slave morality was grounded, for Nietzsche, in *ressentiment*, i.e., the presupposition that weakness is a virtue. In slave morality goodness becomes the safe, useful, or submissive; this morality denies the values that enhance life and affirms weakness as the only moral strength. The attempt here is to manipulate the strong into the acceptance of mass morality through the repression of their former powers and virtues. The weak will attempt to ascend to the higher type, and their slave virtues will have replaced master virtues in rank and worth. The master's virtues have now become "evil," and with this inversion of values there has been a debasement of life for Nietzsche. This moral genesis of the "herd" shows equality becoming the highest norm and dominating contemporary consciousness.[5] The herd animal believes itself to be the highest type of humanity; it has devalued the exceptional person. It will create "the lie of culture" and attempt the further suppression of all those whose values argue for the enhancement of power.

The master morality, on the other hand, refers to the effective imposition of a stronger will as a desirable end. "Master" peoples are willful and strong through the inherent nobility and quality of their preferences. The noble and strong create their own moralities through a power that acts without reference to good or evil or divine sanction. The noble and strong understand the term "good" to mean actions that derive from strength. The term "bad" or "evil" for such a nobility refers only to the fearful behavior of the slave. The strong recognize the values of all slave morality to be the product of *ressentiment,* the resentment by the weak of the superiority and power of the strong. Against this resentment Nietzsche called upon the "higher men" to break away from the herd, and to reveal the dawn of a new day which will affirm that our present nihilistic egalitarianism is only a transitional phase.

Present humanity is for Nietzsche only a rope or bridge between the animal and the overman. As a mass it will never produce a higher individual, but only a species which tends to recapitulate itself. The human species, though, is still the undetermined animal which is incomplete or unfinished in its innermost Being. Out of its incompletion there must come a utilization of the will to power which gives rise to Zarathustra's overman (*Übermensch*). It is the mission of today's higher humanity to counteract the herd's mastery of existence and prepare for a new nobility, for only a noble humanity can establish a noble existence. This higher creature will create new goals for humanity and attempt to instrument new possibilities for the race. These possibilities, the exact nature of which Nietzsche did not spell out, shall be the hope and goal of the human race, especially for higher men. More than a product of evolution, the overman is a creation of human will, in which there will be a dependence only upon human beings; all the transcendent qualities that have been ascribed to God's works will be returned to their human creators. The definition of higher humanity will replace the present dominance of the herd. Its passion for leveling will be exposed as slave morality, and its tendency to equate equality with justice will also be exposed. The overman will provide a "revaluation of values," and the norms of good and evil will be exposed as the themes of the weak. The dominance of the herd will come to an end.

But who and what is this herd? Nietzsche's term "herd" (*Herde*) is his designation for those masses who are in a sort of "left-over" status, i.e., those who still hold nominally to Christian culture in its present secular expressions of equality, progress, morality, democracy, socialism. This herd has arisen, he claimed, from the death of God and transcendent meaning that began with the rise of science in the seventeenth century. For him the term "herd" also designates the accompanying spiritual phenomenon of nihilism as the devaluation of all values into equality. Here the herd legitimizes only those values which it perceives do validate their egalitarian presuppositions. But the values of the herd still spring from a source which the herd does not suspect. The values to which they want others to submit—goodness, equality, selflessness—are actually expressions of the herd's own will to power. The herd will assume that no values can be superior to theirs and that there has never been a collapse of transcendent values, nor even a death of God. They will remain satisfied with themselves as the "last men," the highest products of history. The herd is untruth.[6]

In the twentieth century the whole of humanity will be without direction and in desperate need of re-orientation. That century will be dominated by the secular morality of the herd; and such egalitarian illusions as democracy, socialism, progress, the worship of science, technology, feminism, and liberalisms of all types will be rampant. The herd is the medium of such illusions, the illusions of those who have not fully broken from Christianity yet retain the Christian virtues of "equality" and "selflessness." But at the same time, the herd remains indifferent or even hostile to the theological-metaphysical groundings of the Christian faith. In this sense the herd possesses unclear allegiances. For Nietzsche our present condition demands that the partial break of the herd from Christianity be made complete. If this separation is not effected, the herd's slave morality of *ressentiment* will nullify any possibility of the overman. The herd will always remain within the value frame of *ressentiment*, and the strong will be discouraged from self-creation or self-transcendence.

Nietzsche's assumption here was that the present aims and practices of the herd possess neither adequate worth nor direction for the human race. If the human race is to rise above its present condition, especially herd culture, then the "higher humanity," the ones who prepare for tomorrow's overman, must have the courage to become self-creators, not simply creatures of the mass. To this end Nietzsche wished for the higher individual suffering, self-contempt, and failure, for it is only in such states that the individual proves personal worth. Such worth is not generated by happiness. Instead, worth is more likely the possession of what Ortega y Gasset called the select person, "the qualified minority." Such a person is not simply the one who imagines himself or herself superior to others, but is the one who demands more of himself or herself than the mass does. The radical division of present humanity is not between races, sexes, or classes, but between those higher individuals who make demands upon themselves and those who ask nothing of themselves. These latter are the herd, those who live only as what they are, without effort or self-perfection.[7]

Over against the herd, higher humanity will exhibit the normal tendency of the strong to seek that existence which demands strength to bear suffering and self-creation. It will accept the goal of creating those conditions of society and health that anticipate the overman, who will guide the human race from its present nihilistic condition. This is the master morality of our time. The will to power must be so affirmed that at least the creative minority may be allowed to surpass its present condition and its outgrown Christianity. From the present dominance of the herd with no goals beyond mass culture and decadence, there must be generated higher beings of greater will, strength, and creativity who can accept the demands of life and overcome them. Higher humanity will overcome *ressentiment*. The Christian God will be finally abolished, and the effects of his reign in contemporary herd ideologies will be also abolished. The Christian deity was created to nullify the will to power of the strong. The true human vocation of self-creation through will to power was aborted by a god who was created to destroy the possibilities of humanity. The overman, born of the will to power in the future, must be willfully prepared for in the tasks of today. It is the herd which stand in the way of this creation, this ideal of the overman. Higher humanity must overcome the herd and prepare for a being who is beyond good and evil. Existence must not be feared, but accepted in the context of the hope for self-transcendence. The overman will accept the whole of human existence as it actually is, both terrible and possible; and his or her destiny will be the provision of a new goal and meaning for the earth. The hope of the overman will be the proper response to the present dominance of the herd.

Nietzsche assumed that "nihilism, the most uncanny of all guests, is standing at the door" of the twentieth century, and will persist through the twenty-first. For Nietzsche nihilism is not simply a doctrine which denies any objective grounds for truth or value, but it is the result of the devaluation, after the medieval era, of the highest values into equality with all other values. A vision of higher and lower values became lacking in European society, and what replaced them turned out to be the happiness of the herd as the deepest meaning of life. Egalitarianism, industrialism, and hedonism replaced all aspirations for higher existence. They were implicitly assumed to be the best means of responding to the incipient nihilism of the nineteenth century. Further, the then current ideologies of liberalism and socialism were assumed to satisfy the herd's desire for a life without risk or effort. These conditions have become the grounds of contemporary mass society, yet the illusions of the mass era—God, truth, objectivity, and progress—are over.

For Nietzsche the present world's moral estimate of its significance has devolved into a sort of fiction that avoids reality at
any cost. This estimate is nihilistic at its base, yet egalitarian in
its policies and values. Disintegration is the character of our
time.[8] While the Christian interpretation of the universe
collapses, there is an assumption of total meaninglessness. But
nihilism will prove a transitory phase.[9] This nihilism will be
counteracted by the creation of a new center of gravity in the
form of the overman, who will accept the reality of the will to
power, including the sobering fact of eternal recurrence. Eternal recurrence is Nietzsche's thesis that the world is composed
of a finite number of units which interact in a variety of combi-
nations, so that these will be repeated over and over. That
which is will be repeated, and all that is must be affirmed in its
eternal return. Human life is here affirmed to all eternity, and
it is only the "love of fate" which is able to accept this condition.

In spite of eternal recurrence, the great social issue for Nietzsche is whether human life is of an ascending or descending
type. Today's select humanity will understand contemporary
nihilism and decadence as the fact that the herd principle has
infected both natural rulers and higher individuals. In order to
counteract this herd principle, all public existence must come
to acknowledge the order of rank implicit in the will to power.
This is of crucial importance, for in the present era the disbelief
in the existence of great men will result in the ruin of yet
another people with each passing decade. Social nihilism can be
aborted only through the development of stronger, life-affirming individuals who demonstrate the will to power. Such individuals will judge human goals in accord with their propensity
to aid the ascending forms of human life. Contemporary society, however, is indifferent to either ascending life or the development of higher types. In fact, "modern man" exhibits a
tendency to revert to herd status and abort all higher types.[10]
Unless these tendencies are overcome through an ascending
power, the affirmation of a new goal for humanity, then our
present nihilism will become our permanent possibility. The
will to power is the only means by which this possibility may be
overcome. The power to enhance life is the greatest criterion of
value.[11]

In our presentation of Nietzsche's assumptions it is important to understand that his appraisal of both the advent of nihilism and the herd bore a crucial relation to his conception of Historicality, the unique manner in which human beings are in time. For Nietzsche humanity must be seen as "the incomplete animal" whose potential as a species is dependent upon historical development. Humanity is by nature incomplete and radically dependent upon what-it-is-not-yet. While animals are each perfect after their own kind, human beings are always imperfect in the sense that they remain historical possibilities for themselves. In their imperfection and historical incompletion they will not be finally defined. Only that which has no history can be finally defined. Humanity is not only the product of genetics, and hence self-identical, but the product of self-fabrication in historical time. We will see subsequently that Ortega y Gasset takes up this idea from Nietzsche. For Nietzsche, as for Heidegger and Ortega after him, human Historicality is our own-most property, and as such not understandable only by reference to our present factical condition. Our complete understanding must include reference to our yet-to-be-completed being. It is only the so-called "last men," the creatures of the herd, who imagine that humanity's final perfection is embodied in them. The term Historicality is applicable to Nietzsche's thought, because both his assumptions and his problematic require that we are creatures of the historical process who "happen" in a unique way; i.e., we "happen" as historical becoming. In this sense human beings are to be defined not only as natural phenomena, but as the forms of life whose becoming is self-transcendence. Such becoming is also subjectively significant, because it is experienced as duration, which is immediately lived as the forwardness which connects past, present, and future. In other words, we construct our existence forwardly. For Nietzsche the implication of our historical becoming is that the human being is a *species temporis* which cannot be understood only as a biological entity or a static *species aeternatatis*. The human being is a "happening," a something-to-be-made, and not a something-finally-made. An auto-fabrication by nature, the human being is a drama of self-transcendence which consists of "filling in" its possibilities in the advancement of its life. Unlike animals or natural objects, which remain identical in their species nature and achieve change only through external evolutionary forces, human beings are incomplete creatures which cannot be finally defined. Because incompleteness is at the heart of human being, our existence is seen by Nietzsche to require that we surpass ourselves in time, that our humanity does not remain identical with itself. The new form of human evolution is autofabrication in historical time. Human life is conceived as the possibility for becoming a new being in the self-fabrication to the overman. The revolutionary insights of Nietzsche's on Historicality are one reason he is being reappraised in recent decades as a serious thinker.

(B) Heidegger's Nietzsche: The Issue of Nihilism

For Nietzsche God can no longer be the source of the meanings, values, or perspectives of philosophy. The required philosophical perspective is not one that relates man and God, but one that advances from present humanity to the overman. Self-transcendence to the overman is not for Nietzsche achieved by means of traditional metaphysics, but by an existence that transforms the life values and meanings of the herd. There must be achieved a vision of human autofabrication to the end of the overman. But the great obstruction to autofabrication of the race to the end of the overman is mass nihilism. For both Nietzsche and Heidegger and Ortega this must be understood. None of these thinkers can be completely understood apart from his position on this issue; at this point let us examine Heidegger's response to Nietzsche's philosophical confrontation of mass nihilism.

We can begin to understand this response by noting that after 1935 at the age of forty-six Heidegger began a serious study of the writings of Nietzsche, and he delivered academic lectures on him from 1936 to 1940. His lectures and writings on this subject later appeared as *Nietzsche*, 2 vols. (Pfullingen: Gunter Neske Verlag, 1961). In Volume IV of the English edition of this work, Heidegger discussed Nietzsche's version of both the event of nihilism and the decline of Being in the West. The English edition of this work includes the translation of two lecture courses given by Heidegger at Freiburg in 1940 entitled

"European Nihilism" and "Nihilism as Determined by the History of Being." In these lectures Heidegger concluded his thinking-confrontation with Nietzsche, whom he had come to regard as a thinker of the first rank, the thinker of nihilism who has no peers. Like Nietzsche he confronted nihilism as the fundamental metaphysical issue of our era. Heidegger attempted to show in all his Nietzsche writings how Nietzsche's thought upon nihilism bears an essential relation to the history and destiny of philosophy in the West. Heidegger had come to believe that Nietzsche's will to power was only another form of the Western metaphysics that had originated with Plato. Heidegger attempted to reveal the possibilities of the issues inherent in Nietzsche's thought, and he saw Nietzsche's nihilism as the name for the historical movement which would dominate the century to come—as the fundamental experience of our era. At this point nihilism meant for Nietzsche that "the transcendent would become null, so that all being would lose worth and meaning."[12] From Nietzsche's announcement that "God is dead" Heidegger interpreted his inner meaning to be that the Christian God had lost His power over Being and over the determination of man. Here the term "God" stands for the transcendent in general, for those meanings, norms, and principles which were formerly held to stand above our condition and give it purpose. This transcendence and its secular surrogates—eternality, reason, goodness, natural law, progress, and equality—are dead; they are dead not to the consciousness of the herd but in their final effectiveness or meaning. For Nietzsche it became part of the function of the overman to negate and transcend the traditions that still operate under the assumptions of the existence of God and his secular expressions. These expressions, which were able to sustain a pre-nihilistic age, are in fact fictions which were created to make life more tolerable for the mass. Further, the history of philosophy has been an unfolding pathology which has had as its end the support of a dying metaphysical and moral vision. Its legacy is despair for the present condition. A new affirmation of human existence is required, and this in turn demands a new philosopher who will rise as a liberator like the dawn of day. The philosopher's coming is proclaimed by Zarathustra, and there will be taught a new meaning for the earth. Such a philosopher will be a commander and a legislator, yet this legislator will encourage human life to be an experimental transvaluation of itself.[13] God will no longer be a philosophical issue for the future. But the masses do not yet realize this. They will continue to live out the forms of a religious residue, and continue to participate in the still-extant secular forms of religiosity. They will show little awareness or anticipation of the crises that nihilism will continue to provide.

Yet Nietzsche's interpretation of the advent of nihilism is but part of the whole picture in the thought of Heidegger. Heidegger believed that while Nietzsche had understood the phenomenon of nihilism more deeply than any other, Nietzsche's own thinking was in fact part of the very nihilism he was attempting to expose and evaluate. His will to power is only the last statement of metaphysical essentialism in the history of the West, and as such it is but another metaphysical thesis that informs our present nihilistic condition. For this reason Heidegger believed that the issue of nihilism needs to be addressed from a perspective that transcends Nietzsche's thinking. This perspective Heidegger believed he had found in the question of the history of the meaning of Being. The tradition of Western metaphysics, of which Nietzsche is a part, is over.

We may ask here how this situation came to be. Why is it that Nietzsche's thinking is itself metaphysical, and but the latest expression of an exhausted tradition? How could the "greatest thinker of nihilism" be himself nihilistic? According to Heidegger, when Plato interpreted the question of Being (*Sein*) as form or idea (εἶδος), the fate of Being in the West was sealed. Being was fated to be afterwards understood conceptually as the "whatness" of the world, as the essences of things that are at hand. For Heidegger this Platonic interpretation has come in the West to the position that all Being is to be understood as abstraction or representational idea; there has been a tendency to forget the question of Being-as-such (*Sein*), for Being-as-such has come to be thought of in terms of beings at hand (*Seiendes*). Further, Plato's thought also established that beings at hand were appearances. There is then nothing to the question of Being itself, but the question of the Being of beings; truth has become conceived as the adequation of thought to beings that are at hand. In sum, the crucial philosophical event in the West was the transformation of the question of the meaning of Being itself into the question of the Being of beings at hand. Because of this event, the thinking of the West became metaphysical, and with the rise of Christianity Being-as-such became further re-interpreted as Supreme Being or God. Yet even the Supreme Being was here but a being among other beings, even though these beings received whatever significance they possessed from the Supreme Being. The truth of Being was interpreted as the doctrinal prescriptions of the Church.

For Heidegger the liberation of Western humanity from the dominance of church hierarchy required a new principle of certainty, and a new secular thesis on the nature of truth. It was in Descartes (1596-1650) that a secular but misleading thesis arose. Through his discarding of scholasticism Descartes founded his system on a method of universal doubt. He believed that the grounding of such a method revealed Being as thought and extension. Truth became the thinking ego's adequation of its cognitions to these substances. Clear and distinct ideas became the ground of objective certitude for the determination of beings that are. Subsequently, in Hegel (1770-1831) that thinking consciousness became the Absolute itself, and this Absolute became the final stage in the development of Western metaphysics. But the element of Will as the inner Being of all beings had yet to reveal itself. The Will as the innermost Being of the world became dominant in the thought of Schopenhauer (1788-1860). For him the inner reality of Will appeared as the blind force of striving that governs the existence of both nature and humanity. The resistance of these wills to one another creates strife and unhappiness, and the only resolution for this situation became for Schopenhauer the renunciation of the Will itself. The Will as the chief metaphysical feature of Western thought emerged also in Schopenhauer's successor, Nietzsche. But in Nietzsche Will became the will to power, and he denied Schopenhauer's pessimistic conclusions about the blind force of Will as the inner Being of the world, with his affirmation of the will to power as the essential meaning of human life and the world.

For Heidegger Nietzsche's philosophy was a part of the interpretation of the history of Being in the West. In fact, his
thought was for Heidegger the culmination of Western thinking about Being in the mode of essentialistic metaphysics. Nietzsche had attempted to re-interpret Being as will to power, the
inner nature of the universe and man in it. This Being came to
presence as the will to power of beings, for power was the
ground of all beings. Through his enthronement of the will to
power as the supreme metaphysical principle, Nietzsche
attempted to overcome nihilism as the dominant feature of our
era. But according to Heidegger, Nietzsche's construction
failed, because his position implied that there is nothing to the
problem of Being itself, but only beings conceived as the will to
power. In other words, Nietzsche misconceived Being itself as
the will to power of beings; power became for him the essence
of beings; Being itself was not addressed or understood.
According to Heidegger, this is the very essence of modern
nihilism. Further, Nietzsche held that it was actually the previous faith of the herd in the categories of reason and religion
that had generated modern nihilism, because the herd had
attempted to measure both being and value by the standards of
a fictional world.[14] Yet for Heidegger, Nietzsche's thought was
also inadequate on this point, because he continued to understand nihilism only in value terms. Nietzsche believed that the
question of Being arose in the history of Western thought in
the context of questions about value. Something was designated
as valuable, he believed, only if it aided our striving to power in
the world. Also, Nietzsche's value-oriented thought was never
able to disclose the essence of nihilism, for he saw this phenomenon chiefly in terms of the devaluation of higher values
into equality. But for Heidegger these theses do not reveal the
true essence of nihilism. Nihilism is the result in the West of
our misunderstanding Being in terms of such beings as Nietzsche's "power," or in terms of idea or of God. We must now
examine this claim more carefully.

We may begin analyzing Heidegger's new definition of
nihilism by re-noting that for Heidegger Being itself has withdrawn itself in the West, and the philosophical issue of the
meaning of Being has given way to the Being of beings at hand.

Being-as-such (*Sein*) has remained unaddressed and in conceal-ment. The consequence of this default is that the is-ness of Being has been determined by its staying away.[15] In its aban-doned state Being has been conceived in terms of such beings as power, idea, matter, etc.; and humanity's relation to Being-as-such has been severed. For Heidegger this is the authentic source of nihilism. In the case of Nietzsche, for example, his attempt to think of the world in terms of a being (such as power, the herd, or the overman) is to have misunderstood things for their very ground and condition. Being itself is not will to power, but will to power "is" because it is first grounded in Being itself. Yet Being itself is not thought by Nietzsche. Fur-ther, Nietzsche's metaphysics of the world as the will to power means that power is conceived as the inner essence of man.[16] Mankind here becomes a sort of essence of Being through which the world's nature is determined and measured. Being itself becomes man-centered, and human technology becomes the chief expression of this power. This thinking of Being as human power in technology is itself the deepest expression of nihilism in our age.

But in spite of this, humanity does belong to Being in a unique and important way. It has been Nietzsche's failure, and the failure of the West, not to understand this relation. Human-ity (*Da-sein*) is the there-ness or place of the revelation of Being itself. The essence of man is the abode of Being's event.[17] Humanity is engaged in Being, because from its inception it asks after the nature of Being and its relation to our condition. Through its Being-in-the-world it attempts as human Being to approach Being itself. Authentic nihilism is for Heidegger the denial or forgetfulness of this attempt; it is the false assumption that there is no Being, only beings. While nihilism is usually understood as standardlessness and devaluation, and as the death of God, these perceptions are not the essence of nihilism. Nihilism is the assumption of the nullity of Being itself; it is the attempt of beings in such expressions as the will to power to master Being.[18] However, this nullity of Being, for Heidegger, is not simply something that is base or evil, for the absence of Being is also the preservation of the promise of Being itself. Even in its loss, Being is the unconcealment of its own enigma.

But no matter how the issue is conceived, it is through the loss of Being itself that modern humanity, including Nietzsche, seeks to establish its existence through the will to power as the domination of nature herself. We attempt to compensate for the loss of Being through the technological will to power, which implies the control and consumption of all things. For Heidegger this tendency is dominant in the thought of Nietzsche. His essentialism and humanism have led to the belief that man must replace God as the source of power and value. His will to power is the continuation of the Western proclivity for the dominance of nature. His influence is felt in the modernist assumption that the utilization of technological power must be to the end of an everlasting improvement of living standards for all the masses, regardless of the capacities of the earth. The very destitution of our era is expressed in our contemporary need to be needless and safe, to be self-sufficient beings.[19] The modern will to power demands that we be totally self-creating and self-grounding as the central creatures in the universe. Contemporary ethics, itself nihilistic, is derived from this assumption. Heidegger denied that any such will to power can be the ground of our assumptions about Being; nor can it provide salvation. Instead, to be saved is to be saved from the will to power.

We therefore see that Heidegger's thought upon nihilism is a philosophical dimension beyond that of Nietzsche. He rejected Nietzsche's criteria for the advent of nihilism and attempted to show that Nietzsche's thought was implicated in the advent of nihilism itself. Nihilism is the result of our forgetting of the question of Being in the West; and the manner in which we relate to the question of Being determines our condition upon earth. To evaluate the world in terms of the will to power is to ignore Being itself, to understand Being as an entity among entities. Nietzsche was caught in a metaphysical-valuational essentialism that Heidegger considered a dimension of nihilism itself.

So while nihilism was a central fact for both Nietzsche and Heidegger, they were unlike in their conception of it. Nietzsche's position, in sum, was that the overman must be the creator and measure of all value and meaning; for him the overman would transcend contemporary nihilism and its herd through the affirmation of the will to power. When the human source of the creation of value and meaning had become hidden, through the herd's creation of a transcendent realm of "truth" and "goodness," then this condition in turn hid from humanity the ideal supremacy of the overman and the will to power. Nietzsche considered the will to power to be the ground of all valuation, the fundamental Being of the world, and the criterion for the goals of humanity. Nietzsche's "herd" was the majority of men and women who do not or cannot recognize these facts, those who cannot live with the will to power, and who require for their lives the transcendent power of the "beyond." The overman would will a higher humanity over against the herd; the overman would redirect humanity away from its wandering over the earth.[20]

For Heidegger, on the other hand, the thinking that is required for our time of need will abandon the will to power. Our openness to Being is neither willed nor powerful, but a "gift to man." We are free in our letting be and in our release-ment (*Gelassenheit*) to Being, not in possessing or forcing anything. Heidegger considered Nietzsche's thought, along with that of Hegel, as the end of metaphysics. Nietzsche saw Being as a being, a power. His thought could overcome neither nihilism nor the herd which lives in nihilism's world. His metaphysics possessed no superiority over the tradition of which it is the last exemplar. Everything for Heidegger depends upon our conceiving Nietzsche's philosophy as the end of metaphysics in the West. We must replace it with a "releasement" into Being as the "silent power of the possible."

This search for the truth of Being led Heidegger to the poetry of Hölderlin and to the study of language. Language became for the later Heidegger the house of Being, a home in which man dwells. Whoever thinks or creates in words is a guardian of this dwelling. Being comes to expression in both language and poetry. For the later Heidegger human existence was no longer the starting point of his thinking. Instead it is our "releasement to Being" that becomes the crucial fact about humanity. Human Being's end is not the will to power, nor the mastery of nature, but to become the "shepherd of Being." We

exist not to dominate the earth by the power either of the technological mass or of the overman, nor to dominate by representational theory, but to guard and express the truth of Being.
This is our authentic life.

(C) Heidegger: The Mass as Technicity

We have seen that Heidegger's "anybody" (*das Man*) possesses
both an affirmative and negative significance. In the affirmative
sense, the "anybody" is a mode of Being-with in the world, a
positive constitution of Dasein, in other words the public way
we are in the world with others. It refers to the way we cope,
expect, and judge in a situation which is already socialized. The
"anybody" here is the pre-thematic or implicit way we exist as
more than the I-myself. This common or public world belongs
to us and governs our interpretation of ourselves and our experience. As a source of usages and assumptions, the "anybody"
makes the discovery of entities other than itself, both shared
and coherent. Dasein, then, is a sociality that both assumes and
comports in a common world. While Dasein's own-ness is in
each case the "I-myself," the "I-myself" is for the most part a
being-with. For example, whether we speak of a baby's use of a
spoon, or consider the child as affectionate or strong, we interpret the child in relation to a social context, a relation that
implies others. The child as Dasein also comes to understand
itself in terms of its "care" in a public world. Put another way,
Dasein understands itself in part through its care-ful participation in meanings, language, and uses which are also cared for
by others. Dasein's "doing" is in significant part a common
doing, a common expectation of meanings, purposes, and eval-
uations that are cared for and shared. Dasein, then, encounters
itself in a public world of social coping and purposive behavior.
Being-with (*Mitsein*) is thereby an essential part of our Being-in-
a-world.

Yet for Heidegger, as we mentioned above, there also is a
negative sense of Dasein's Being-with as the "anybody." The
"anybody" is an authentic sociality as positive constitution, a
source of public meanings and expectations, but it also
possesses a defective or negative sense. The latter is a perma-

nent possibility of Dasein, and a state in which Dasein participates by various degrees. The defective sense of *das Man*, the
"anybody," is encountered when it serves not simply a form of
social intelligibility or expectation, but when it exhibits a
dangerous abandonment of both freedom and responsibility for
itself. Hubert L. Dreyfus has argued that the "one" or
"anybody" here is a defective "conformism." Here it is not
simply our necessary social conformity, but that which slides
into a state of falling.[21] The "fallen" one exists in a specifically
identifiable state of conformity that nullifies the person's
authentic possibilities. It is the purpose of this section to show
that the defective "anybody" is to be understood not as Nietzsche's "herd" but as the technological mass of contemporary
society. While Nietzsche's doctrine of the will to power was a
necessary prelude to Heidegger's understanding of it as the
technological domination of nature, our contemporary state of
massification and nihilism is due to our complete forgetfulness
of Being. In his essay "The Question Concerning Technology"
Heidegger defined technology as "nothing technical" but as the
disclosure of all beings as raw material for exploitation by the
human subject. Here the will to power has become the mass
movement to understand and regulate all beings as sources of
energy and consumption.[22] This situation came about not
through human will or decision but through our misunderstanding of Being itself as the will to power. The essence of
technology is the conception of Being as power and the human
will to power. In this sense "technology is nothing technical,"
and its sense of human reason has become the faculty for the
representational thinking and domination of the earth. This
situation has presented contemporary humanity with a "world
night," a night so destitute that present humanity cannot see
beyond technological Being. The origin of our present mass
nihilism is our inability to understand ourselves in a world in
which the forces of technology are equated with Being as the
will to power.

But Heidegger presented an even more specific picture of
the modern technological mass. In his essay "The Age of the
World Picture" (1938)[23] he claimed that the mass is equivalent
to that human movement which competes for position to orga-

nize the technological world picture for private ends. In other words, the mass (*das Man*) in the defective sense refers to those who blindly submit to the will to power for the technological-economic domination of the earth. *Das Man* becomes here the mass falling into the conformism of planetary economic-techno-logical imperialism. In this state the end of humanity is conformity to one unconsidered possibility, the economic-tech-nological will to power. The highest norm it can proclaim is the unqualified ever-higher consumption of goods by the world's masses. This state is dressed out as "higher living standards," a state which assumes instant approval. Here we have a techno-economic nihilism that demands of present-day humanity a fall into its confines, an unthinking adherence to its internal norms. The "anybody" has here become not so much a source of public meaning and expectations of our Being-with others in a world as the conformism of *das Man*.

Heidegger saw the fall of *das Man* into its defective states as part of the crisis of all modernism. Unlike Nietzsche he under-stood this crisis in terms of the West's forgetfulness of Being. But it is also important to realize that his evaluation of modern technology developed in the context of a more general German resistance to modernist ideas and to the late arrival of industri-alism in that land. Such contemporary thinkers as Ludwig Klages, Oswald Spengler, and Ernst Jünger participated in what came to be called the *Streit um die Technik* (The Controversy over Modern Technology). Heidegger was considered part of this movement, but he claimed that our contemporary crisis could not be understood simply by reference to economic, historical, or technological elements alone. He located the ground of the crisis in what he would call "productionist metaphysics." By this he meant that the inner being of modern technology becomes more and more hidden from the human observer; and our present mass culture, unlike Nietzsche's presentation of it, cannot be distinguished from the present manner in which we relate to technology. The striving of the technological mass, as we suggested, is for increased living standards, security, and equality in consumption. Indeed, in sensate-industrial modernism, equality *is* equality of consumption.

As a self-willing power the technological mass is the contemporary expression of the will to power and not to any other destiny or form of life. In this thinking Heidegger was greatly influenced by the then-contemporary German philosopher of technology Ernst Jünger, whose treatise *The Worker* (*Der Arbeiter*) became an important source in the technology controversy.[24] For Heidegger Jünger's writings revealed most clearly the metaphysical state of the West at the end of the metaphysical era. Jünger maintained that neither Marxist nor liberal theories could explain the inner nature of industrial technology in the twentieth century. Industrialism is but the outer form of a deeper configuration which he called the "*Gestalt* of the Worker." Jünger argued in this formulation that the emergence of the modern worker can only be understood as the expression of a latent will to power. This will to power of modern nihilism he specified as "the total mobilization" of productive power to the ends of mass consumption and economic security. The modern world, said Jünger, must submit to the so-called *Gestalt* of the totally mobilized workers. This means that modern technology cannot be avoided or stopped, but only endured and lived through. Such an inevitability is the result of a force beyond itself—the will to power. Technology must actualize the will to power into the creation by the worker of standing reserves for future consumption. Heidegger came to believe with Jünger that the twentieth century mode of Being is technology as a world picture. We can transcend its chaos and violence only through our understanding of it as the destiny of the West. We are released from its control only in our acceptance of its power. Heidegger would replace Jünger's technological will to power with his thinking upon Being, but he retained Jünger's concern that the mass will be reduced to a calculating animal. With Jünger he saw our modern experience of Being as the belief that beings must be transformed into the possibilities only to calculate and stockpile for the gratification and furtherance of the will to power for the domination of the earth.

For Heidegger this is the possibility that is most relevant to the nihilistic destiny of the West—that technology will decide the destiny of the masses, but never the reverse. Present leveling in modern society takes the form of prohibiting individual possibilities, i.e., of insuring that the modern individual is no longer in charge of things or of his or her individual destiny. According to Jünger's thesis of the *Gestalt* of the worker, human beings are identified not as ends in themselves but as raw material to be utilized for stockpiling and the furtherance of power. This means that the craving for power has become an end in itself, a process with no purpose beyond itself. The answer to the questions, "Why are you doing X?" and "What value does it have?" has become, "Because I am doing it." (For example, "Why do you want a higher standard of living?" . . . "Because it is a higher standard of living.") Here is total nihilism and massification, for not only are alternative ends not possible in this technological destiny, but the question of alternative self-direction may not even be understood by the individual. Because human beings can be totally identified as raw material to be utilized for "stockpiling" (e.g., for developing more consumer goods), our Being has become what Heidegger termed *Gestell*, enframed or constricted in our possibilities. Dasein's openness to Being has been lost, and our dependence on Being is forgotten. The common-sense ideology that the control of nature through the will to power is the only source of happiness reinforces this technological nihilism. There then grows the widespread assumption that the saving powers, to free us from our conformism, are not present in our time.

For Heidegger the authentic posture that we may take toward this era is not the earlier notion of resolution (*Entschlossenheit*) of the *Being and Time* period. Instead, for the Heidegger of what is known as his later "turning" phase, it is "releasement" into the actuality of things (*Gelassenheit*). While society accepts nihilism, the mass, and technology as the present disclosure of Being, we must nevertheless stand apart from this situation, and in our standing apart we must remain open to Being. In the later Heidegger this openness to Being is understood as "releasement" to that which is beyond the will to power, as a waiting for the new disclosures of Being. Calculating thinking must be replaced by an attitude of thankfulness (*Danken*). Human πρᾶξις or reason cannot attain this releasement. Present productionist metaphysics has forgotten the Greek sense of τέχνη as the disclosing or producing of something previously hidden, and it tends to misconstrue creation or disclosure as material causation exclusively. There must be revived the sense of production as the art (τέχνη) which lets something be in its openness. This letting-be is the proper end of poetry in the present age, for poetry resists the technological understanding of Being.

In sum, the technological mass in our present era has so restricted the possibilities of humanity that its only authentic possibility seems confined to the defective sense of the public "anybody," the average assumptions and intelligibility of technological culture. Dasein may choose to flee into such a mass so as to disguise from itself the nothingness that it feels at its ground; or it may assume only those roles as its own which are available to it in econo-technic-culture. In such roles Dasein will tend to understand itself only in terms of those possibilities that the mass allows, and other possibilities will be forgotten. The role of the "hero" who discloses and embodies new possibilities will be nullified; the individual will no longer even repeat historical possibilities, for there will tend to be a forgetfulness that our selfhood is rooted in Historicality, and there will be a tendency, in the face of the technological present, to forget the Historicality of humanity. This will be the case even though technology will be seen by the mass as the vehicle of all change and progress.

(D) Kierkegaard, Nietzsche, and Heidegger on the Mass—Comparison and Contrast

For all three of our thinkers the status of the crowd is a vital philosophical and moral issue, and a central problem for our modern age. They described the problem in many ways, but often used similar terms, such as Crowd, Mass, Herd, or *das Man*. One aspect of the problem, as we have seen, is the conformity or tyranny of the Crowd, whereby the individual loses sight of his or her possibilities or worth, freedom or responsibility, actuality or authenticity. A second aspect of the Crowd is its "leveling" power and its assumption of abstract equality of all persons and equality of all values, such that both persons and values are de-valued and meaningless. A third aspect is that individuals become numerical units, statistical abstractions, whose anonymity devoids them of importance or responsibility or concern. A fourth aspect is the Crowd's tendency for spectation, for idle talk and curiosity, for passive participation in public events, for a blurring of distinctions between public and private, for avoidance of authentic (either-or) decisions. Fifth, the "Crowd is Untruth" in terms of "deifying" itself, deceitfully presenting itself as an idol, whose followers are superior to any non-members, and deceitfully posing as the savior of humanity, through the socio-political-economic-technological "progress" it supports. That technological *Gesellschaft* dominance of our present age is a focal issue of its own, upon which our three thinkers both agree and disagree, their agreement being on its negative power to destroy individualism, to create a pseudo-safety zone to which the individual can flee from anxiety, to destroy traditional *Gemeinschaft* communal relations, to impose herd values which debase mankind, to exploit human beings as raw material for stockpiling and consumption and domination of the earth, and to deceive us as to our authentic goals and possibilities. The three thinkers unite in condemning Nihilism in our era, but differ as to its causes and implications.

Let us then summarize similarities and differences between the thinkers with respect to the causes of our present era's danger or disintegration. All three pointed to the questionable power, historically, philosophically, and morally, of the Enlightenment, and the corresponding unquestioned allegiance to objective "truth" formulated on the assumptions of the natural sciences, rationalism, lawlike behavior, and abstract norms of ideal, secular equality. Secondly, all saw the negative effects of technological industrialism. At the same time, all three realized that the domination of the Crowd and corresponding weakness of the individual is partly caused by the weakness, fallenness or incompleteness of the very nature of the human being; all described human being as "in process," as becoming, and as auto-fabrication, with the negative consequence that there is a constant temptation and possibility for each of us to be less than we ought, to flee our responsibilities, to let the crowd act for us, or to deceive ourselves as to values and goals. It was Kierkegaard from whom Heidegger borrowed the fundamental assumptions (expressed in *Two Ages*) of *das Man*. However, for Kierkegaard *das Man* always retained the defective sense of the crowd; it was always a state of fallenness, dispersion, and inauthenticity; whereas for Heidegger, as we know, *das Man* is both the positive and negative or defective aspects of our Being-with, our existential Being-in-the-world; Dasein for him always includes the sociality of public uses and meanings, because we are limited to the contexts of public order and history—we cannot and do not define ourselves *solus ipse* in a private world. Nietzsche, by contrast, referred to the limited, finite possibilities of our perspectives, to the historical undermining of our powers by the Socratic repression of the Dionysian outlook in favor of Apollonian rationalism, and to the historical development of Judeo-Christian slave morality. Both Kierkegaard and Nietzsche criticized the Christian church, in practice, for its promotion of bourgeois secularism, mass behavior, and devaluation of individual responsibilities to abstract equality. Nietzsche, of course, proclaimed the invalidity of God and all trans-mundane salvation, while Kierkegaard maintained that the foundations of Christianity are essential keys to individualization. Both Kierkegaard and Heidegger differed from Nietzsche in perceiving that one root cause of the entire problem of the Mass is the philosophical distinction between existence and essence. Heidegger borrowed from Kierkegaard the thesis that the self must be understood as that entity which comports itself to itself; that the self is essentially a relation to its self; the self has no final givenness to itself as a complete or self-evident substance—it is existence before essence, and is a process of subjective experiences constantly being assembled. But it was Heidegger who interpreted the problem of the Crowd most fundamentally as one of Ontology, of Being, as opposed to beings-at-hand; we have seen his criticism of both the Christian theology and Nietzschean will to power as metaphysical illusions that confuse beings for Being, though the Christian answer is God-centered, while Nietzsche's was man-centered.

We could continue to elaborate differences in the three thinkers about the causes of our modern predicament. For example, we could again credit Kierkegaard for his insights on the power of the press or media, and for relating the doctrine of Envy to the leveling of the Crowd. He too differed from the others in his interpretation of the stages of human life and history, as well as his conception of human falling and faith. And we must again note that the Mass and Nihilism became a focus for Heidegger only in his later thought; in the period of his *Being and Time* he was concerned with the everyday existence of Dasein in its relation to Being, and not with the problem of individuation per se; his account of the everyday self of Dasein recognized resoluteness and authenticity, but the phenomena of leveling and falling, he said, can only be understood in ontological analysis.

At this point we need to summarize both similarities and differences in what the three thinkers considered to be the necessary response or solution for retrieving the individual from captivation by the Mass. While the differences are often glaring and obvious, the similarities are more impressive than may be expected. All three emphasized the importance of the individual becoming a self, being authentic, and actualizing or fulfilling his or her possibilities. The task of becoming a self is the great end of human life, as Kierkegaard affirmed; it is the major, lifelong task, for we are always in process of becoming, in anxiety, fear, and trembling. In Nietzsche's eyes we must seek a higher humanity, which will set new goals for the whole human race, by having the courage to become self-creators. In Heidegger's terms we must stand apart from the defective or inauthentic behavior, be aware of our true Being, and be open to its possibilities. By what means can we achieve this individuality or self-creation or authentic Being?

First, for Kierkegaard the engines of the self are choice and will, and these propel us through different spheres and stages of the self's actualization; the stages on life's way cannot be reduced to or explained from the mass order—their denominators are in the individual personality, who must make either-or decisions, whether they be on the level of aesthetics or ethics or religion. Obviously, Nietzsche too put top priority on the engine of will, the will to power which is the inner essence of man. Heidegger did not stress the terminology of will, or Kierkegaard's terms of commitment, passion, or ultimate concern, but he referred to Resoluteness as the first means of retrieval—the call to the self, the self taking hold of itself, or being "vigilant for Being."

Secondly, there is a similarity of means in the role of anxiety or suffering; i.e., the very struggle to become a self can force us to awareness and decision. Kierkegaard wrote of fear and trembling and dread or despair as intimately connected with the leap of faith that can actualize our possibilities. Nietzsche proclaimed that self-worth is generated not by happiness, but by failure, contempt, and suffering—and the strength to bear and overcome them. Heidegger categorized Conscience, Guilt, and Anxiety over our imperfections as three means that force us to look at what we have become or not become. He also elaborated on the Care Structure that is so essential to our nature —the constant concern about our status as human beings and about our possibilities.

A third common source for actualizing our individuality is a genuine relationship to other individuals. Kierkegaard reminded us that while we cannot return to the feudal *Gemeinschaft* community, Christ's love is the model for a life of faith and the basis of human relationships in a true Christian community. As we said earlier, for Kierkegaard our relation to the eternal is partly social and communally related, by virtue of the primacy of *agape*. Further, in the attempt to become a "single one," we must reach out to un-deceive others, and preach as well as practice the inward mode of existence, even to the point of martyrdom in ministry to our age. For Nietzsche, while the "free spirit" lives alone, he or she works to create a higher humanity, whose existence will not be selfish, individual power so much as the creation of new goals and possibilities for the whole human race. One of Heidegger's words for the kind of commonality or sociality in which we preserve our individuality is Solicitude, the competence of Dasein to be with others understandingly. But it is also Heidegger who stressed Heritage as playing an important role in our retrieval of the self from the mass, for "authentic possibility can never be separated from our heritage and community," and only through our past associations and traditions can we create our future.

The very fact of Death and our finitude seems to be a fourth common source of awakening the self to its possibilities, in the face of no possibilities. Because of man's "sickness unto death," his "infinite despair" and "despair of finitude," Kierkegaard took on the personal life mission of counteracting it and showing humanity a way out. Nietzsche connected the strong individual with what he called *amor fati*, the acceptance of fate and affirmation of struggle. And Heidegger specifically addressed death as a means of making us realize we are separate from the mass.

Finally, an unknown or quasi-mystical realm plays a role for all three men, necessitating either Kierkegaard's faith, a leap made in fear and trembling to the eternal, or an open-minded waiting, in both Nietzsche's and Heidegger's writing, for a higher humanity, the "overman," or a revelation, disclosure, or "clearing" of Being itself. All three hoped for a future age of greater, more authentic possibilities for mankind.

There are obvious differences between our philosophers as to solutions for the problem of the Crowd. For Kierkegaard the individual can be finally saved from the nihilism and massification of modernism only through the Christian *telos*, never through secular or rationalistic means. Christ is the salvational paradigm for humanity, and it is through Him, in a leap of faith, that our worldly condition is transcended; we cannot actualize or individuate ourselves apart from a relation to God, because our human finitude and sin are such pronounced elements in our existence. If we place our reliance upon the public, socialized, and secular perspectives, we shall devolve into despair, the sickness unto death; *das Man* is always a state of fallenness, dispersion, and inauthenticity. The choice, through passionate inwardness, of the Christian religious experience provides our final and highest self-determination and individuation; but the modern individual is not able by his or her own effort to escape the leveling of the public order—one cannot escape anxiety or despair through the power of personality, reason, or will alone—by themselves they will lead to the suspicion that authentic choice is impossible, that an existence before God is impossible. But for Kierkegaard the religious life is still not precluded. In his examination of what he calls "Religiousness A" the individual is seen to die to the secular and finite, to attempt to achieve the eternal in time. This tactic is supposed to provide to the individual the continuity and strength to counteract the dispersion and leveling of modernism. But at this level of faith our choices and actions often contradict each other, and the individual again falls into despair. At this point the individual may ascend to "Religiousness B," the achievement of perfecting individuation through the model of Christ. At this level through the emulation of Christ we do a new thing, and the eternal is created in the temporal. For Kierkegaard this is the most authentic posture that the individual may take in the face of nihilism and the crowd's untruth.

For Nietzsche all salvational themes in Christianity are beyond hope or pertinence; all hope is placed in self-transcendence and the overman. Nietzsche's thought remained secular and naturalistic to the end. His thought was humanistic, but extended to the farthest reaches of human possibility. We can never transcend the personal, finite perspectives through which the world is given to us. Philosophy and religion are creations of the weak to mask the terror and tragedy of existence. If we are strong, we will accept and affirm the human condition, with all its chance, danger, and tragedy; like the ancient Greeks we will create a synthesis of the ideal and the real, the sensate will and the rational restraint; we will demand the most of ourselves, and provide a "joyful wisdom" revealing that "our present nihilistic egalitarianism is only a transitional phase" leading to the creative, courageous "revaluation of values" in the overman. Our Historicality and autofabrication, as a species which constructs its existence forwardly, make such a future self-transcendence possible to us.

Heidegger significantly assumed Kierkegaard's existential problematic and Nietzsche's analysis of nihilism as the fundamental metaphysical issues of our era; but, as we have shown, he could accept neither Kierkegaard's individuating and salvational elements nor Nietzsche's man-centered will to power, itself trapped in Platonic metaphysics and contributing to the very problem of technology which causes nihilism and the destruction of the earth. For Heidegger the way out of our problem is, first, to understand the everyday existence of Dasein in its relation to Being. Dasein must always be understood in the context of the existential *Mitsein* of the public "anybody" or "they"; we cannot exist apart from our makeup as a being-with; our very existence requires public uses, meanings, languages, and customs in sociality and history; this status is radically secular, and Dasein cannot be "unworlded" from a public "anybody" of pre-assumed interpretations and social roles. Dasein is individuated as something unique, but is that existence which defines itself to itself in the appropriation of a public and historical world. Whereas Kierkegaard's self is a spirit, a synthesis of body and soul, with the capacity for self-transcendence in God, Heidegger's self is existence.[25] Authentic human Being is not something apart from the "anybody" or *das Man*, as it is for Kierkegaard; it remains in all its possibilities an essential modification of *das Man*.[26] The self must be created from the social and historical forms which are factically available to it.[27] Heidegger tended to see final individuation always in terms of the finitude implied in death, for we are our final identity as beings towards death. Kierkegaard's prescriptions are grounded in theology, Heidegger's in ontology. For Heidegger Dasein's orientation can never be trans-mundane salvation, and there is no possibility of eternal meaning and unconditioned existence. Fallenness is not only inevitable, but a state of our everyday Being. In this state we flee from anxiety into the pseudo-safety or everydayness of the crowd, utilizing social presupposition and the model of *das Man* for the attainment of our identity.[28] There is no final *telos* for Dasein. Yet an authentic life is possible, and we are enjoined by Heidegger to be resolute, self-defining, and open to responsibility for our decisions. Further, Heidegger seems to be unique in providing us with two more means to the authentic self. One is the posture of *Danken* (thankfulness) instead of *Denken* (thinking), together with the sense of wonder at existence, the wonder, for example, that "There is something rather than nothing." The second is τέχνη, the disclosure or "letting something be in its openness," which we find in poetry and in openness to the question, "What is the meaning of Being?"

Kierkegaard was the founder of Christian existentialism and Nietzsche of atheistic existentialism, two schools which exist to this day. Yet both thinkers were alike in their concern for the importance of the individual in the impersonal crowd. Both thinkers in a sense came too early for the nineteenth century they addressed, but in the early and middle twentieth century they were taken up, and their thought exercised a critical import for psychology, theology, literature, and social criticism. Heidegger was the legitimate heir of both thinkers, but exceeded them in his strict and formal ontological analysis of Dasein in the context of the whole problem of Being. All three were outstanding spokesmen for our modern predicament, the massification of the individual, a fallenness for which we seem born but from which we may find retrieval. All three were critical of the failure of modern philosophy and religion to help provide that retrieval—failure out of fear of the subjective and passionate or inward nature of existence, or failure out of enslavement to beings-at-hand and to out-dated scientific, secular, rational assumptions about our Being. All three perceived the crucial importance of Temporality and Historicality in the very makeup of the self and in our ability to understand and create ourselves. However, the most famous analysis of the masses in our century is that of the Spanish philosopher José Ortega y Gasset, to whom we now turn.

PART THREE

JOSÉ ORTEGA Y GASSET

Chapter Five

Ortega y Gasset and the Idea of Human Life

(A) Ortega's Life and Circumstances

José Ortega y Gasset was the son of a leading editor and lawyer in Madrid. This precocious child, who was to become the greatest critic of the masses in the twentieth century, was born in 1883 into the culture and privilege of the liberal upper classes. The young Ortega attended a Jesuit school which grounded him in Latin and Greek and granted him a bachelor's degree at fourteen. Later he would criticize this classical education for promoting pedantry and shyness in the young. He went on to study at the University of Madrid and received his *licenciado* in philosophy and letters in 1902. He was granted a doctorate degree in 1904 at the age of twenty-one, having been examined for this degree by Miguel Unamuno. His later concern with historical crisis was anticipated in his dissertation *Los terrores del año mil, Crítica de una leyenda* ("The Terrors of the Expected Millennium"). The young scholar believed that the Spain of his youth was intellectually and culturally provincial, and this attitude graduated into one of the themes of his life. He came to believe that his mission was to bring European culture and institutions to Spain, a mission that was not endorsed by his teacher Miguel Unamuno (1864-1936). In 1905 Ortega went to Germany to begin post-doctoral studies at the University of Leipzig. There he studied Kant's *Critique of Pure Reason*, a text he considered the earmark of all claim to philosophical competence. He also studied experimental psychology under Wilhelm Wundt (1832-1920). In 1906 he gained a scholarship from the Spanish Ministry of Instruction to continue his philosophical education at the University of Berlin. The following year he attended the University of Marburg and plunged himself into the neokantian movement led by Hermann Cohen and Paul Natorp. Critical of the whole of speculative metaphysics, these thinkers would direct Ortega to the area of philosophical methodology, especially the methodological distinction between the *Naturwissenschaften* and the *Geisteswissenschaften*. At Marburg Ortega learned of the incipient phenomenological movement that had been inaugurated by Husserl about seven years previously. While he was initially impressed by this movement, and considered it as a foundation for his own developing philosophical position, he would later correct this early estimate and orient his thinking to the life philosophy of Wilhelm Dilthey (1833-1911), whose empirical subjectivism he would consider the major principle of his later idea of human life and the current philosophical era.[1]

After his marriage, and some further study in Marburg in 1911, Ortega returned to Spain, where he attacked his former teacher Miguel Unamuno for his *hispanizante* (Hispanicist) sympathies with the Spanish traditionalism. He succeeded to Nicolás Salmer's chair of metaphysics at the University of Madrid in 1911, and he remained in this post until 1936, when the Spanish Civil War commenced. He published his *Meditations on Quixote* in 1914, and he later claimed that in this work his idea of human life was first outlined.[2] He founded the sociopolitical review *España* in 1915 and became active in the Political Education League, which would later mature into one of the elements of Republicanism during the Civil War. Two years later he founded the newspaper *El Sol*, which he hoped would objectively reflect the Spanish national situation. In 1921 his publication of *Invertebrate Spain* (*España invertebrata*) provided a famous critique of what he considered the supine tendencies of Spanish national life. The year 1921 also saw the beginning of a series of lecture courses which he would later publish as *The Modern Theme* (*El tema de nuestro tiempo*), a book often considered the fullest representation of Ortega's thought. In 1923 he founded the leading philosophical and cultural journal of Spain, *Revista de Occidente* (*Review of the West*), which he published until the outbreak of the Spanish Civil War in 1936. The journal was later revived, and it continues as a distinguished Spanish publication to this day.

Ortega had come to maturity during a period when Spain was undergoing both chaos and national guilt over the loss of the Spanish American War. The nation possessed neither organized leadership nor national purpose. Spanish national life seemed to the young Ortega both negative and unreal. Science and learning had declined and the national educational system was in need of extensive reform. The so-called Generation of '98 was a group of writers and critics which had previously attempted to examine Spanish national life in essays and novels. The group included the writers Ramon Perez de Ayala and Miguel Unamuno. But their influence was no longer a force in the nation, and the Spain of Ortega's youth was "the sick man of Europe." Ortega came to believe that it was the mission of his generation to reconstruct the main lines of Spanish civilization into greater conformity with European education, politics, and culture. In his *Invertebrate Spain* (1921) he argued that the Spanish masses existed without an elite that could exercise the political, moral, and educational leadership that was so greatly needed. He also believed that there was no effective counterforce to Spanish traditionalism, and there was need for the Germanic model of culture and science (*Wissenschaft*) to act as the educational model for higher education in Spain. Ortega, in other words, was a critic of the *hispanizantes*, who would govern Spain through the appeal to culture and tradition. For Ortega this "Africanism" of traditional Spain could never guide the country into the contemporary era, and he supported the leadership of the *europeizantes*, who would strive to reform Spain after European models. But it is important to note here that Ortega also wanted to preserve the higher elements of traditional Spanish culture, which he believed could be integrated into the European science and technology of the twentieth century. To this end he and others founded "The School of Madrid," a group which included Ortega himself, Manuel Morente, Xavier Zubriri, José Gaos, José Mora, and the foremost of Ortega's disciples, Julián Marías. This School was held together by the ideology which proclaimed that education, higher culture, and politics are the means for the re-orientation of Spanish life in the twentieth century.

In 1929 Ortega resisted the dictatorship of General Primo de Rívera, a person Ortega considered the very embodiment of the mass man, and he continued to publish his *Revista de Occidente* during his rule. He resigned his professorship to protest the closing of the university by the dictator in 1929. But he continued his philosophy lectures before large audiences in a local movie theatre on the subject, "What Is Philosophy?" After returning to his university post he continued to lead republican opposition to the dictator's regime. In 1930 he published his *Revolt of the Masses* (*La rebelion de las masas*), a work which graduated him to world fame. This work is the main focus of our present study. At this time he was elected deputy in the constituent assembly of the Second Spanish Republic, and he became the leader of a parliamentary faction called "In the Service of the Republic." When the Civil War opened in 1936, he was forced into various exiles. He went to Paris during this period, and he was subsequently offered a position at Harvard University, which he refused. He accepted the invitation of the Dutch historian Johan Huizinga to lecture in Holland in 1938. He later went to Argentina, where he passed the last half of World War II at the University of Buenos Aires. Here he began his most important sociological work, which was published posthumously in 1957 as *Man and People* (*El hombre y la gente*). Returning to Europe in 1942, he lived at Lisbon and founded a publishing house. He would return to Madrid on occasion, but he was prohibited by the Franco government either to teach or to participate in politics, and he enjoyed no rights at the University of Madrid. In 1948 he and his disciple Julián Marías founded in Madrid the Institute of Humanities, which was subsequently closed by Franco. Isolated from the national life of Spain and greater Europe, Ortega attempted to counteract his political situation by attending world conferences. He came to Aspen, Colorado, in 1949 to attend the Goethe Congress, and he also visited England and Germany, where he defended the idea of European Union. His final years were spent in a schedule of travel and lecturing. He was awarded honorary degrees from the Universities of

Glasgow and Marburg. Ortega then met Heidegger at Darmstadt, but such high points became increasingly rare in his career, and the last years of his life were darkened by mental depression, disappointments in his projects, and regret that he had not developed his philosophical positions in a more technical manner. In 1955 he died of cancer in Madrid at the age of seventy-two. Contemporary Spain had lost her greatest son.[3]

In his *Revolt of the Masses* Ortega held that "select" or excellent people always orient their lives to standards which are superior to themselves. But they gladly serve those standards, and they refuse to remain either identical or satisfied with themselves. While Ortega served the standards of philosophy, literature, journalism, politics, and education, he never developed a formal philosophical system, or school, nor did he carry out an examination of formal philosophic problems in technical monographs. Yet he had important philosophical disciples, and he contributed greatly to what has come to be known as the philosophy of human life (*Lebensphilosophie*), a school largely founded by Wilhelm Dilthey (1833-1911), a thinker whose work Ortega appropriated and developed importantly in his own right. Ortega's thought parallels and amplifies many philosophical themes of Friedrich Nietzsche (1844-1900) and Martin Heidegger (1889-1976), but his thought is significantly different from these, and imports an originality of its own.[4] Albert Camus remarked that "Ortega y Gasset, after Nietzsche, is perhaps the greatest European writer, yet it would be difficult to be more Spanish." While his writing is confined to the extended essay, he managed to achieve an intellectual depth and clarity on many philosophical issues, including the nature of human life as fundamental reality. For Ortega the end of human life is to provide meaning and clarity to a world that is constantly losing its orientation. He attempted to provide to contemporary thought a grounding in what he called "the radical reality of human life." Human life is the philosopher's ultimate concern; and human life in our era is in desperate need of a principle which is objective to itself; in addition, there is presently required of our thinking a new comprehension of human life in historical time.[5] But what is this doctrine of human life? How can we read its primal text? It is this issue that we must now examine.

(B) Human Life: The Text of Reality

We shall attempt here to introduce the main lines of Ortega's philosophical position, especially his idea of human life as radical reality. This general section will then serve as a prelude to his thinking upon the phenomenon of the masses as a form of human life. There are many ways that we may speak of the phenomenon of human life. We may, for example, speak of it as the biological status of plants and animals, the opposite of death. The young Ortega used the term in this way in 1911, when he discussed life as a biological concept in an article on Jakob Uexkull's *Umwelt und Innenwelt der Tiere*. But this is not the sense that he would suppose when he claimed in *The Idea of Principle in Leibniz* (1958) that the leading idea of his philosophical maturity was human life. The term was here used to refer to the dynamic interaction between the "I" and its circumstances, a polar relationship between the interiority of the self and the surrounding world.[6] Human life is given to itself not as a theoretical or scientific conception, but as a pretheoretical reality through which we exist and appear to ourselves. We are whatever our life is and nothing more. Human life is radical reality, he claimed, because it is prior to all other realities, and all that we call real must appear within it. Ortega expressed the polarity of human life in his famous phrase, which itself became a sort of philosophical battle cry: "I am myself and my circumstances" (*Yo soy yo y mi circunstancia*). Circumstances are the other half of our Being. Circumstances are everything in which we find ourselves and through which we compose our Being. The "I" must always refer itself to a world-component or an intentional object apart from itself, and of which it is aware. The "I" also encounters itself as a pure interiority, for as Ortega put it, everything that perceives itself from within is an "I."[7]

While human life is the most fundamental reality that is given to human beings, it is always experienced as my life, the life of each one of us. We are fundamentally our own life, and this life can never be reduced to or explained from any object at hand. Because it is the polar reality of "I and circumstances," it can never simply be perceived externally, but only lived from within as my own. But it is easy to be confused about Ortega's meaning here. He did not mean to claim that there are no other realities than human life, e.g., matter, God, the universe, ideas, etc. Rather, he wanted us to realize that these usual candidates for radical reality are actually of a secondary nature, because they never appear apart from the meanings, history, goals, values, and explanatory devices of human life itself. Human life is prior to these other realities not in extent, power, or even rank, but because all that we call real must appear within it. It is in this sense that human life is radical reality.

Ortega discussed his idea of human life in many of his works, and he remarked that it was implicit in his early *Meditations on Quixote* (1914) and even as early as 1910 in his "*Adan en el Paraíso*" ("Adam in Paradise"). But it is in his posthumous book *What Is Philosophy?* (1957) that Ortega provided what is perhaps his most adequate single account of the phenomenon of human life.[8] He asserted that human life is not something that can be perceived apart from ourselves. It is in fact what we are, what is happening to us, and what we are doing with ourselves. Our existence is transparent to ourselves, and in this sense our self-possession. But we possess our life under the requirement of having to do something with it. We must carry it forward in time by living out of our past into a present, and toward a future. This temporal "I" is not a completed thing, for it is always presented with circumstances with which it must deal and construct itself. The "I" is presented with what Ortega called "unabsorbed circumstances," and the very process of human life is the bestowal of order and meaning upon those previously unabsorbed circumstances. Human life "becomes" not through its "I" alone, but through the things and significances that it must address to become at all. Human life is that becoming which constitutes itself through something else. Unlike a self-contained object such as a stone, which is encapsulated in itself without concern or orientation to circumstances, the process of human life is always to be worked out in relation to those things about which it must concern itself. Also as a concern-ful being, which exists as "I and circumstances," human life cannot be understood as spirit, matter, or substance. Because it is never an eternal but a finite being, human life is self-constituted under the aspect of circumstances (*sub specie circumstantiarum*). For these reasons Ortega sought to supply a new significance to the term "reality," and he did this by showing that human life as radical reality replaces the traditional philosophical conception of Being. Since the presocratics, especially Parmenides, Being has been presupposed as the real, as whatever is in and for itself, as that which most truly is. It has traditionally been opposed to all "becoming," and for this reason the ever-changing process of human life has often been assigned to the status of the sub-real. For Ortega Being must now be assigned to human life, an entity whose very essence is process, and we must further examine his reasons for doing this.

In his 1929 lecture course entitled "What Is Philosophy?" Ortega devoted himself to a fundamental analysis of the nature and claims of philosophy. The basic thrust of philosophy since Descartes, he claimed, has been the construction of a theory of knowledge in the face of the rise of science. But, as Kierkegaard, Nietzsche, and Heidegger also noted, such an emphasis has exercised a negative effect upon human life, for since the rise of natural science in the seventeenth century, human life has been relegated to the status of mere subjectivity. Only the mathematically quantifiable properties of matter in motion have been considered ultimately real. Human life has remained a "secondary quality" whose status is ambiguous. Further, as we have said, ever since the time of Parmenides Being has been postulated as the fundamental term of all that is (ὄντος ὄν).[9] While Ortega had the tendency to dismiss the classical theories of Being as fictions, he also, like Parmenides, understood Being as that which truly is. But in his *Some Lessons in Metaphysics* he required that the term only be applied to the radical reality of human life. Our human life is not only our innermost being, but the real ground in which all other realities appear.[10] This understanding of Being conforms to Aristotle's stipulation that any adequate usage of the term Being must also include the temporal element of the "act" of being (ἐνέργεια ὄν). Ortega's stipulation that human life is a "becoming" accommodates this requirement. At the same time Ortega's assigning of Being to human life excludes the Parmenidean notion that Being is static, for Ortega's human Being is radically historical and self-constituting. Yet Ortega's formulation also complements the Parmenidean notion that Being is the status in which all contingent and secondary elements must appear.

Any attempt to ascribe final Being to such timeless metaphysical entities as the Parmenidean "One" must be rejected. Being can no longer be confined to timeless realities. Such attempts have only tended to "seal the fate of Western thought for 2000 years." From its genesis in the thought of Wilhelm Dilthey, the idea of human life has been the governing assumption of our era, and the new concept of Being must be limited to the temporal reality of human life. It is only the idea of human life which places a proper priority on process. Ancient and medieval thought had placed emphasis on the metaphysical formula *operari sequitur esse,* by which was meant that the identity of something depended upon the prior nature of its Being; that actuality precedes possibility. But the idea of human life as radical reality reverses this formula to the contrary one of *esse sequitur operari*; i.e., the nature of an entity can only be understood as the cumulative stages through which it has passed. This latter formula is the modern one, and the construction of human life in time is especially relevant to its more recent reformulation. Human life is here understood as the Being whose deepest nature is process and development. As such the tendential structure of human life must be understood as "a gerundive, not a participle, a *faciendum,* not a *factum.*"[11]

It must also be noted, at least in passing, that Ortega believed that his idea of human life as radical reality had corrected yet included the traditional philosophical positions of both realism and idealism. He attempted in his idea of human life to replace both of these as viable philosophical schools. The realist position has held since the Greeks that the objects of sense and cognition are real independently of their being apprehended or thought. According to Ortega, realism was the fundamental assumption of both Greek and Medieval thought. Reality was for them independent of its being perceived or thought by a subject. The prototype of the real was considered to be a thing, a *res* whose manner of being is independent of all subjectivity. The realist thesis was contradicted by idealism, the dominant school since Descartes. Here it was maintained that reality was not only subject-dependent, but mind itself. In its extreme forms the Being of something was its being perceived (*esse est percipi*). In Descartes (1596-1650) thinking became substance itself (*res cogitans*).

Ortega attempted to replace both realism and idealism by a more inclusive perspective upon the real, and this new perspective is the idea of life as radical reality. Here neither the thesis of the primacy of mind nor the thesis of independent existence is adequate to the philosophical needs of our modern era. The authentic philosophical comprehension of the real must surpass both realism and idealism and penetrate to the radical reality of human life. Neither the primacy of realism's "thing" nor the pure inwardness of idealism's "self-consciousness" is able to express this reality. There can be no "outside" dimension of the real apart from the inside of a knowing subject; nor can the subject exist enclosed upon itself without reference to a circumstantial world. The real must be composed of both an "I" and a "not-I." In his *What Is Philosophy?* Ortega argued that an independent world can be adequately constituted only in conjunction with a subject for whom it is significant, and the real can be neither the indwelling immanence of idealism nor the pure outsideness of a thing unintentionally related to an "I." Human life alone is both indwelling and transcendent, and Ortega believed that his idea of life as radical reality was able to salvage the partial truths of realism's claim that the real must refer to an objective world, and idealism's claim that the objective pole of experience is always an object for a subject. Subject and world are together in such a manner that they cannot be separated by abstract philosophical, scientific, or logical methods. The radical reality of human life cannot be confined to a subject or an object. It can only be understood as the bi-polar reality of "I and my circumstances." Apart from the artificial bifurcations of realism and idealism these poles have never been separated in the actual existence of man. Ortega expressed this togetherness of world and circumstance in his contention that the human being discovers itself only in a world, a world that has a meaning for a subject. I am aware of my life as both a continual receiving of the world and a concerted action upon the world. These actions and reactions reveal to the human being how he or she is in the world. Our being in the world is for Ortega a "shipwreck," a problem to itself from the beginning. This means that human life does not exist simply as an actuality, but as a possibility for itself. Not only are we forced to be in one circumstance or another, but we are forced to choose among them as we advance into the future. The being of our life is never resolved in advance of itself. Life's circumstances and temporality consist of the fact that we are always on the way from a past to a future. This future to which we advance is a future upon which we must decide. Human Being is a radical becoming in historical time, a *species temporis*, never a *species aeternitatis*. Such a temporal status implies for Ortega that "Human life possesses no nature, only a history." To understand this claim it is necessary to understand two things: the Historicality of human life and the historical reason through which it must be comprehended.

The term "reason" has a checkered history, but Ortega meant by it any act of the intellect which brings us into contact with reality.[12] According to Ortega, there has been a tendency in the history of philosophy since Descartes to restrict the designation of the term to the inferences of logic or to the generalizations of the physico-mathematical sciences, what Ortega called physico-mathematical reason. These thought forms have since tended to be considered the most authentic paradigms for all discursive thought. But Ortega's philosophical thinking after about 1929 would remind us that the Latin root *ratio* refers to any attempt of the mind to grasp the inner principle of widely different phenomena, and the end of all human reason is the provision of behavioral and intellectual criteria for the attainment of our ends in the circumstantial world (*saber es saber a qué atenerse*). Prior to 1929 Ortega focused upon an alternative to physico-mathematical reason which he designated as vital reason (*razón vital*). This new reason, the thought form required for the comprehension and explanation of human life, was to be the *órganon* which explicates the processes of human life. Ortega had argued as early as 1924 in his essay "Neither Vitalism nor Rationalism" that all reason is rooted in human life, and not transcendentally derived from "pure reason" or from physico-mathematical thought forms. In his "vital reason" we have a thinking which mistrusts both rationalism and any such irrationalism as the vitalism of Bergson, Driesch, and Spengler. His program of vital reason was to be the explanation and clarification of human life in circumstances. [13]

But subsequently in his career Ortega tended to replace this "vital reason" with another thought form, which he called historical reason (*razón historica*). It is clear from Ortega's 1928 lecture series "What Is Philosophy?" and his *Man and People* (1939) and *History as System* (1941) that the concept of historical reason came to the foreground of his thinking during that time. While vital reason never entirely vanished from his philosophical usage, it clearly gave way to a new expression that could address the radical Historicality of human life. This change was due significantly, but not entirely, to the influence of Wilhelm Dilthey on his thought after 1929. It was from both Dilthey and Nietzsche and Heidegger's *Being and Time* that Ortega came to believe that the temporality unique to man is Historicality and not cosmic time. [14] It was also after 1929 that Ortega's strong socio-historical interests began to show themselves in such works as *The Revolt of the Masses* (1930), *Man and Crisis* (1933), *An Interpretation of Universal History* (a 1948-1949 lecture course), and the posthumous *Man and People* in 1957. All of these elements combined to produce in Ortega a new thinking that could address itself to the reality of human life in time and circumstances.

Historical reason can be understood in Ortega's thought not only as the thinking of human life in circumstances (vital reason), but the thinking of human life as radically historical. For Ortega Historicality is the thesis that man has no nature, but a history. This is to say that for Ortega there is a difference between our biological and our biographical life. Since his *Meditations on Technology* the idea of human life as biography, as a story in time, had been a crucial element in his thinking. In this work he indicated that the category "my life" is not merely a biological one but a biographical one. Further, from about 1923 in his *El tema de nuestro tiempo* (*The Theme of Our Time*) to *En torno a Galileo* (*Man and Crisis*, 1933), Ortega had seen the problem of philosophy to be the thinking of human life in its biographical dimension. This position rests upon his prior claim that our biological or our "species" nature (*homo sapiens*) is a scientific abstraction which began to develop about the time of Aristotle. But this species nature is not human life as it is actually experienced by man. The organs, nerves, and structures of our biological life are not the radical reality of human life, but secondary and ostensive realities which appear within it. Human beings were their lives before they were biologists, and even biological science and its objects appeared within a specific period of human life's past. While our biological existence is of course a necessary condition for the possibility of human life, it is not the condition for human life as radical reality.[15] What I do or what happens to me is a feature of my biographical life. My life is not my cells, nerves, digestion, locomotion, or secretions. Rather, these biological phenomena appear within the course of my life. Even my body is not my life, but it is an objective circumstance within the uses of my biographical life.

Yet human life cannot be separated from its biological dimension, our species nature. The human being is both natural and extra-natural, both biological species and biography. We are, in Ortega's words, "ontological centaurs." Man is at once both his biological nature and the "extra-natural" being which is biographical life. Put another way, we are creatures composed of organs, cells, and nerves, which proceed without our consent or direction. They are in this sense self-realizing entities which appear within my life. But my "extra-natural" being, my biographical life in historical time, is not ready-made, or aside from my consent or direction. The biographical existence of my life as radical reality is a self-fabrication which accumulates itself forwardly in history. It is this human being, this "ontological centaur," which grounds Ortega's assertion that "human life has no nature, but a history." Our biographical life, never fixed, is always faced with the demand to become something which presently it is not, namely its future. Our circumstances demand that we fabricate our life to future circumstances, that we create ourselves in time as history. It is in this sense that we come to realize that technology is not something incidental to our lives, but a component of our very self-making. Technology is human life's utilization of the circumstances through which we fabricate our lives. In fact it is, for Ortega, in our reaction to circumstances that we attain our extra-natural human status as biography. Ortega meant by this that we are self-fabricative beings who are "creatures in need." We exist in unfavorable or problematical circumstances that must be constantly transformed, and we must "earn" our being in time. This being is the "drama" of our lives as self-fabricators. Self-fabrication forms our biographical being in time. In other words, we are what we do, and what we do composes the story of our life. We are by nature historical beings.

Our biographical life is a paradox. The paradox consists of the fact that our existence is at once an actuality and a possibility. We are an existence into our future; what we have not yet become cannot be separated from what we are in the present. We are always bounded by our own incompletion. Because we are always in need and always lacking what we might be, we are forced to construct ourselves, and it is this fact which makes us radically historical beings. Our Historicality is what we are, and what we are is incomplete. While the drama of our life is incomplete, it is yet our only possession. But it is possessed as a temporal species, never a *species aeternitatis* removed from its own Historicality. Human life is a historical happening, a *res gestae*, and the thinking and the explanation of this happening is historical reason. Historical reason is the thinking of how human life fills in its present with its future. It addresses the fact that we are "not-yets" who must always surpass ourselves in temporal circumstances. Because this history is the very reality that we are, our life is the story of how it has achieved itself in time. This awareness that our Being is a being-in-time brings us to the recognition that our history is the only reality that we completely possess.[16] This radical Historicality of human life was first proposed by Wilhelm Dilthey, but Ortega went beyond both Dilthey's Historicality and his critique of historical reason with a variety of historical reason that was his own. This historical reason became for Ortega the dialectical method of the radical reality of human life (*Realdialektik*). In historical reason we have a description of how we emerge in time, and how we invent our lives in circumstances. In his historical reason Ortega completed the *Realdialektik* to which Dilthey devoted his life.[17]

The "dawn of historical reason" is for Ortega the new instrument, the new thought form that can address itself to the fact that history is the real ground of our existence. From 1933 to 1935 Ortega was advancing this conviction in his *Meditación de la técnica* and *Historica como sistema*. Human life, he claimed, can only be grasped by a thought form that addresses the Historicality which is at its base. This is historical reason.[18] In other words, historical reason is the attempt to narrate how human life happens to itself, how it constructs itself in time. Historical reason is the narration of life's biographical dimension, its story. Ortega expressed this fact in the claim that "Narrative reason is historical reason."[19] This formula presupposes the position of existential phenomenology that phenomena reveal their truth in time. In this case the truth of human life, what it is, how it was composed, is expressed through temporal narration. As the *ratio* of human life in time, historical reason provides the most complete and immediate account of the radical reality of human life. The method is autonomous in that it does not derive its methods or assumptions from realism, idealism, or physico-deductive models. This reason is for Ortega a new era of thought, "the dawn of historical reason." Previous thought forms have all ignored, forgotten, or repressed the Historicality of human life. They have either treated human life through the methods and materials of natural science, or they have forgotten the biographical dimension of our existence as accumulation and autofabrication. Also, physico-mathematical reason, for purposes of our existence, has collapsed, and historical reason, the thinking of human life as history, has replaced it as the theme of our time.

But there is another dimension of historical reason that is crucial to Ortega's position, and this is the prediction of the forms of human life in the future. If historical reason is to be adequate to the understanding of human life in time, then it must in some sense address the future. This future-oriented explanatory element Ortega understood as "self-eternalization," the attempt of life to possess the future through foresight, prediction, or prophecy. An example of the self-eternalization of human life in prediction might be as follows: since human life can anticipate definite goals and the behavior which approximates them, it is the case that contemporary human life can now anticipate a future of checked or unchecked population growth. We may presently forecast, at least in a tentative manner, the probable effects on food supply, environment, and human quality, if this growth continues unchecked. We can also fabricate those practices, norms, and institutions requisite for the probable reduction of this growth. While the forecasting and fabrication of these means remains problematical, the ability of reason to anticipate realities is not nullified because it is problematical. Historical reason can become a sort of instrument that anticipates the possibilities of the future in conjunction with definite practices that would promote certain possibilities and exclude others. The historical reason thesis claims that we are responsible for the future in the sense that human life possesses in its development the power of self-alterability or autofabrication. In other words, we are technicians with respect to our human life in time. We are technicians who are responsible for the future through the autofabrication of human life. The final phase of historical reason, then, is human autonomy with respect to the future, and the anticipation of future circumstances. History is here seen as a "system" of past and future relations in which our technological self-construction is central. It is a system of relations between present and past actualities and future possibilities. It is the understanding of our life in time. We must now turn to the import of this for the rise of the masses in Ortega's thought.

Chapter Six

The Mass as the Dominant
Perspective of Our Era

(A) Authentic Sociality

We can recall that our human life as radical reality is a life that is transparent to itself. In this sense our life is individuated and self-enclosed. But other lives are also a vital fact, and our life is a co-existence, a being with others in which I am a circumstance for them, and they for me. The relation of this other to me and I to the other is not simply an external bodily relation, but a reciprocal presence of two inwardnesses.[1] This other is at once an external body and an inwardness, and Ortega called this dual status an alter ego. This ego may be encountered as an individual or an impersonal collective. The appearance of this other, this alter ego, is a circumstantial fact with both positive and negative consequences. On the negative side, the alter ego may be a restrictive and dangerous fact in that it may turn upon me and afflict me. Such a negative possibility—or in fact any apprehension of social contact—mandates that my behavior must at least partly be exteriorized, and this exteriorization Ortega called *alteración*. This means that I am required by others, and they by me, to become altered away from the immediately personal and interior life which I live as an individual. The term *alteración* will be given a more complete meaning in this section, but for now we can note that this state is not an abnormal one, and it is only meant to indicate that our life is social, that it must go outside itself to the other.

A second feature of our co-existence, beyond the necessity of *alteración*, is our acceptance of common usages. As in Heidegger's *das Man* existential, in so far as we would survive in social circumstances, and in so far as we are creatures in need, we must conform to the other's usages and expectations. This other is the embodied inwardness (individual or collective) whose expectations and roles we must infer and apprehend. To conform to those expectations and roles of the other is not simply an obligation for us; it is also a positive feature of our circumstances. Our individual lives are not possible in a vacuum, without the social and economic framework of the world. This social framework is not haphazard or random, but is confined to what Ortega called the usages (*vigencias*) or practices that are in force in our social circumstances. These *vigencias* refer to the customs, laws, norms, traditions, beliefs, and expectations which inform and dominate the social collectivity. These *vigencias* are not arbitrary or artificial, but binding on the individual. They are always "in force," because the others who compose our circumstances are, like us, always in problematical situations which demand social resolution. For Ortega these social forms, these conformities, are culture, the accumulations of the techniques and artifacts by which man has confronted the problematical circumstances of a given era. Incidentally, of course these social requirements always conceal powers which can be used for us or against us. And cultures, as well as individuals, can rise or fall according to their social problem-solving techniques. Ortega pointed out that while a culture is able to adjust to problems, it is viable and alive; but when it can no longer respond to circumstances, then the culture will fall into a failure of belief and action and disappear.

In his important sociological work entitled *Man and People* Ortega described the social order—the usages and meanings of our being with others. The agents who compose this social order Ortega called the "people."[2] The term "people" here is a sort of generalized other, a fiction that is half real and half unreal. Sociologically the "people" refers to the fact that a large part of our individual life is composed of usages that are not simply the possession of the individual, but of the groups as a generalized other, or alter ego. This is Ortega's way of indicating the concept of *Mitsein* that we noted in Heidegger—that human life is largely, though never entirely, composed of matters that are required of us in social conformity. Most of what we do and expect refers to behaviors and significances that are comported, not because they belong to us on our own account, but because they are socially available or "done" in the culture. In this sense our lives are not simply self-creating or individuated. The "people" is here an agent who can require of us those actions and significances that are social. Further, as we live our individual lives, and orient ourselves to circumstances through our estimations of what is real and valuable, we find that our behavior is not unique, nor "ours alone." Most of the usages, beliefs, and expectations by which we conduct our lives were never thought up on our own, never derived from ourselves, nor were they derived from evidence or theory. We think, behave, believe, and expect in socially common ways, because these are presupposed and expected by the "people."

This "people" collective is a necessary and positive element of our lives, a basic given that makes sociality possible, even though the "people" is always an impersonal collective, a sort of stranger which Ortega called "the implied agent of the passive voice." This agent is at once a sociological construct, yet a part of our individual selves. It is an agent not in the sense that it is alive or objective, but as the entity which acts as a repository of uses, beliefs, and all the requirements of sociality itself. For Ortega this "agent of the passive voice" is also linguistic, in the sense that its uses correspond to those of the requirements of the natural languages, when they refer to the anonymous collective; for example, the *on* of French, the *se dice* of Spanish, the *they* or *one* of English, or the *das Man* of German usage. In an expression of the anonymous collective, such as "they say," or "they are not wearing that anymore," there is an implied agent who has some force and normative authority, yet who is nobody in particular. It is an agent who does not exist in space and time, yet seems to refer also to everybody in general. Of course this collective-agent voice is not simply linguistic alone, for it is an important aspect of our personal and social being.[3] This usage is ours as a constant possibility of our thought and behavior; and under normal circumstances this "one" or "they" as an anonymous collective is nevertheless something which each individual can detect upon reflection and distinguish from him or her self. Here the "invisible, indeterminate, and irresponsible agent subject" is the "people," society, or the collective "one." It is recognized as what we do, think, or expect in social usages which are not derived from our individual authority. It is what is expected by the "people" when the individual "I" ceases to operate and social necessities "take over my life." When this happens, I become in a sense "outside of myself," and I seem to occupy another agency. Yet this situation, Ortega claimed, is the normal way in which we are "socialized."[4]

While this people-collective is a form of our human life, it is not a "group soul" which enjoys a metaphysical status above the individual subject. The collective can never generate thoughts or actions; the individual generates these. Yet the collective has a real status in the sense that it is a characteristic of the way individuals act, think, or speak in terms of social reference. In this sense the collective is a property of ourselves. The "people" is a positive and necessary entity, for it is the ground of our socialized existence; without the common assumptions of collective usage the individual could not survive in social circumstances.

In this chapter we have looked primarily at the authentic, positive side of our human sociality, our co-existence that demands normal "exteriorization" (*alteración*) and conformity to social customs as accepted, collective techniques of problem-solving. But there are many degrees, along the scale from positive to negative, in the way the social order or the people-collective affects our individuality. For example, the handshake is a socialized, polite behavior which can be intensely positive, personal, authentic, and satisfying; or it can be merely a willing gesture; or it can be an automatic, social reflex with no particular personal association; or it can be a phony act in which one is conscious of the insincerity or desirous of rebelling against it, etc. Ortega refers to such an ambiguous social act as "infrahuman." Even though our socialized behavior is capable of affecting us in a most positive and useful sense, the collective can also dissolve the individual into a sort of mechanical or animalistic status in which no individual subject seems responsible for what is done, thought, or said. We have behavior, in other words, for which nobody is responsible, yet all presuppose and use. The handshake is always performed by individuals, for whom it may be meaningful; yet this behavior is social or collective in the sense that it is also a mechanical and traditional expectation of the anonymous "one" of the collective. One performs and usually benefits from this action, and the handshake, for example, is utilitarian and normative, yet "nobody" is responsible for its significance as a social entity. Its meaning and its life are trans-individuated. This usage is at once one's own, yet it is a property of the collective one. It belongs to us as individuals, because it is also a group possession. It is not our own creation or responsibility as a usage, yet it is our own as an individual performance.

Like all properties of the infrahuman people-collective, this usage may at times be understood as "mechanized," "soulless," or even tyrannical. The handshake is traditional and authoritative, and often without authentic intent, akin to such automatic and often soulless greetings as "How are you?" when the question is answered by an equally mechanical "I am fine." This behavior seemed to Ortega an example of an intermediate stage between that which is actually personal and that which is "merely natural," like a physical reflex. It is individual or personal in the sense that the individual person elects the usage, but it is naturalistic and mechanical in the sense that it is habitual, somatic, or unreflective. It exists under the form "I do X because it is done, because it is usual." What is "done" or "usual" here is the representation of the infrahuman "people" or "one."

This "one" or the "people" is then everybody and nobody. Its usages, meanings, and expectations are not actually individually willed or authorized, but they exist in a collective way. The "one" is an infrahuman "somebody" who is "nobody," and it becomes a "somebody" only because it is a "nobody." But it is important to remember here that this infrahuman creature, the collective people, is also ourselves. It is ourselves at least in the sense that it is a constant possibility of our individual being. But this infrahuman creature who demonstrates collective behavior may at other times be an individual agent who thinks, acts, or values on his or her own account. The individual may in one case presuppose the usage of the handshake, but in another case refuse to perform it, or may make the hand into a fist. We may accept social conformities, but we may also refuse them. We may even create new usages. In so far as we can appropriate some possibilities and reject others, we distinguish ourselves from the "anybody" self. By refusing behaviors or enjoining other alternatives, we may also behave creatively, individually, or freely, apart from the expectations and assumptions of the collective. When we are in this sense authentic "I's" who act out of an agency which is our own, and on our own account, Ortega signified that the "I" has regained its individual humanity: my actions are intelligible to me, I know what I'm doing, and I desire to accomplish something on my own part.[5]

At this point we may pose several questions. If the human being is a unique individual, then how does he or she become an infrahuman collectivized one who acts out of an agent that is "outside" the "I myself"? How then can our collectivized self regain its individuality? What is the relation between the two states? Ortega addressed these questions in his *Man and People*, as we noted above, but he also addressed them in 1939 in an informative and important essay entitled *"Ensimismamiento y alteración"* or "Being In and Being Beside One's Self."[6] We must now turn to this essay, for it is crucial for our understanding of both the authentic sociality of the people-collective and the authentic personality of the individual. We can recall that the radical reality of my life is at once my own personal possession and a co-existence with others. The "other" is not only an external body, but an alter ego with its own inwardness. The other may take the form of an individual or a group or collective, but it always remains part of the circumstances by which I must regulate my behavior. In this sense my life as radical reality is not simply my personal being, but a co-existence which is also a collectivized and exterior possibility of myself. This means that my individual self is not only able but even required to go out of its original status as my own interiority to the other for its uses and possibilities. This going out from myself to the other, this merging of our own individuation with the collective "one," Ortega designated as *alteración*. This term is derived from the Latin *alter* or other, and he meant to indicate with this term that one of the authentic forms of our life is its integration into the other, the collective. The collective "one" is an inevitable and useful component of my life, a constituent through which I must express myself, and deal with circumstances as a social being. Here the collective other is my authentic sociality, a part of my being that I cannot do without. It is that which requires that I go outside of myself in order to be myself.

But there is another sense of my "going outside of myself" which is negative and problematical for life. This is the defective sense of the collective "one." Here the "other" is a dehumanizing possibility of myself, an impersonal and authoritative state which removes me from myself as an "I." It can take from me the power and will to originate my own actions and blur the intelligibility of what I do. It can replace the ends I supply to myself with the ends of the "one." In this condition I am in danger of dissolving into the other, not just in terms of the common usages and expectations that our authentic sociality demands of us in our being with others, but in terms of losing even the fundamental residues of the self. I may come to live entirely in the expectations and conformities of the other. In this case my "I" has become more or less captured in a situation or group from which it cannot distinguish itself. If this happens, I have become dehumanized and made into an automatic component of the expectations, uses, values, and meanings of the other. My "I" has been captured in defective *alteración*. In assigning myself over to this negative type of *alteración* I have escaped from my freedom into an unfreedom. To the extent that this happens, the individual self that I have autofabricated becomes empty, and dissolved away from its own creations, meanings, and responsibilities. My life is no longer my personal creation, but a sort of abdication to the other. This abdication is not simply the authentic assignment of part of my life to social and public uses, but the assigning myself to a "one" who is not my own. While it is my destiny to have the other compose part of my circumstances, and to conform to the uses of the other in normal *alteración*, I am in its defective condition so outside of myself that I have lost the ability to distinguish myself as the individual that I am.

On the other hand, the internal state of our own-ness, which may be retrieved from restrictive *alteración*, Ortega called *ensimismamiento,* a term derived from the Spanish verb *ensimis-marse* or "to withdraw into oneself." The individual is here able to *ensimismarse,* to retreat to his or her interior world, where it is possible to suspend the governance of the collective uses of *alteración.* Here the individual takes a stand from within. Here it is possible to define ourselves to ourselves, to come to terms with what is definite, with what we believe or reject for ourselves. From within, in *ensimismamiento,* I may abort the quiet frenzy of the collective other, and better detect where the other ends and my "I" begins. *Ensimismamiento* is Ortega's rejection of the contemporary tendency to be intent only on what is outside ourselves. It is the attempt to live apart, to refuse to be possessed by the other.[7] It is Ortega's means of salvation from the mass.

Unlike the animal, which lives outside of itself and is governed by what is outside itself, the human being can find a place to withdraw within; the human being can free itself to think upon its circumstances. In thinking about its circumstances it creates "margins of security" for itself. This thinking of security and providing for it is what Ortega called technology. The human technician from within formulates ways of dealing with circumstances in such a way that they do not dominate human life. From *ensimismamiento* the person fabricates a self which he or she did not possess before. A new self-relation to the environment emerges, and the individual from within attempts to bend the world to his or her personal program. In so doing the individual "humanizes" the world. For Ortega this humanizing goes through three stages. At stage one the individual in the face of circumstances feels "shipwrecked" in a world and resigned to a negative state of *alteración.* In the second stage the individual withdraws into *ensimismamiento* and forms ideas and plans for circumstances and programs for future actions. In the final stage the individual returns to the outer world and carries to it a plan upon which he or she acts. This is the stage of human πρᾶξις,[8] the utilization of thought for the humanizing of the world.

If we are frozen at the dehumanizing stage of *alteración* and lose the capacity for inwardness, we can cease to be free human agents, and we can allow ourselves to be assigned to the other as an inert mass. The mass is that collective state which is always outside of itself. Not only is it indifferent to the authentic "I," but it resists any of our attempts to autofabricate the self. Always content with itself in the face of circumstances, it confines the individuated self to the infrahuman. Ortega's contention here is that in the face of the mass we must construct our humanity, not simply in terms of biological development, but through what we do with our lives in historical time. It is this Historicality of human life that lifts us above the animal scale. The mass, the state of being totally outside oneself in the collective "one," prevents both *ensimismamiento* and the autofabrication of our life in circumstances. Because the mass is always inert or self-satisfied with respect to standards above itself, it prohibits the self-creation of those who would live apart from it; it prohibits the retreat of the individual within; it requires that its members remain outside themselves. It is in this defective state of being outside ourselves that we, singly or collectively, fall into a state of demoralization. Demoralization is the inability to fabricate ourselves in circumstances; it is a state in which self-creation becomes impossible. It is the mass. And it is to this phenomenon that we must now turn.

(B) The Revolt of the Masses

In his *Man and People* we saw that Ortega characterized the collective "one" as a form of life that is infrahuman, mechanical, and external, a sort of intermediate stage between humanity and nature. In the positive sense this collective may be understood as the "people," his term for the regular, predictive behavior of the group. This people-collective is the means through which we participate in the traditions, uses, and requirements of culture; it is the authentic sociality of the human being, the legitimate and necessary way we are with others in the circumstantial world. But for Ortega there is also a defective status of the social collectivity, and in his 1930 work *The Revolt of the Masses* (*La rebelion de las masas*) he designated this state as the "masses." In this work he attempted a phenomenological description of this mass as it arose in history and as it presently exists as the dominant social and moral phenomenon of our time. We must now attempt to see what this mass is.

In *The Revolt of the Masses* this collective is a negative entity, an object to be detected, defined, and criticized, and if possible circumvented. Ortega began this work by informing the reader that the masses exist, and that the purpose of his book would be to form a moral and social typology of their existence. He went on to proclaim that "the masses by definition neither can nor should direct their personal existence, and still less rule society in general . . ."[9] The implication of this pronouncement is that both Europe and the Americas are suffering from a crisis in their civilizations. This crisis has a name, which he called the rebellion of the masses. Yet this crisis is not primarily political, for it also possesses moral, economic and intellectual dimensions. While the existence of the multitude or the "many" is not new to the West, the mass is a phenomenon that begins in the nineteenth century and continues into our own.

Prior to this time the multitude was composed of many divergent groups with wide differentiations from each other. The principle of inclusion in these groups was the special purpose or ideal to which they devoted themselves. Ortega gave as an example of this the Knights of the Order of Malta or the Knights Hospitalers. These were the religious order of St. John of Jerusalem. Their special end was the care of pilgrims in the Holy Land in the eleventh century. They also had the end of driving out the Saracens from Jerusalem. The coincidences of this minority group with other medieval groups were secondary and apart from their main purposes. Each medieval social group wished to separate itself from the multitude of others, and each stressed its points of separation.

But in the modern multitude, which Ortega designated as the mass, the individuals share an important identity or commonality with the individuals of all other groups, namely their participation in the mass. In our era the mass multitude is not separated by unique purposes or ends, but includes all sub-groups with itself. In the mass there are over-arching characteristics which all members share in terms of their moral and psychological makeup. This commonality is so pronounced that from the presence of one individual we can detect the massification of the whole. For example, one characteristic of the mass is that the individuals of all groups "set no value upon themselves," and have no great concern over that fact. Unlike the example of the Knights Hospitalers group, this group of "just alikes" does not compose itself for special purposes, but passively rests content to be identical to an undistinguished multitude of others. This new multitude is not a particular class, race, or sex in a polity, but a social average that crosses over all groups.

Ortega's mass represents a great division in contemporary humanity, similar to Nietzsche's distinctions, between those who make no demands upon themselves, and those who do. This division refers to those, on the one hand, who are content to remain identical with themselves, who demand nothing of themselves, and who have no perfection of vision or action; and those, on the other hand, who do strive to raise standards for themselves and the human race. This division does not occur, as it is usually assumed, between distinct socio-economic classes, but between the self-transcending and those who cannot or will not understand themselves in terms of a "hierarchic separation" of effort, ideals, or excellences.[10] Those who succeed in interpreting themselves in these ideal terms are for Ortega "the specially qualified." Those who do not are the unqualified. Previously, the ones who required of themselves such special excellences were also the ones who believed that certain vocations required special excellence and effort, e.g., artistic or political-leadership careers. Presently, the unqualified, the unselect, aspire to all vocations and ranks, supplanting the qualified minority—yet they do not cease to be a mass. In the coming of the masses we experience the victory of what Ortega called "hyperdemocracy," the belief of the commonplace mind that in such matters as art, intellect, or politics it has the right to impose itself where it will.

The phenomenon of the mass is a "brutalization" of civilization, a degradation new to our time. Our civilization is brutalized, Ortega believed, because in its deepest nature all society is aristocratic, and a society can exist only to the extent that it is aristocratic. When in society this deepest nature is perverted by the assumption of automatic equality, and effortlessness or self-satisfaction, then it is brutalized. Of course Ortega's norm is not the traditional aristocracy of Versailles or the present English monarchy, but that of the self-perfecting and critically responsible individual. The modern problem is that such an individual is cowed by the fact that the masses are demanding positions and functions that were previously restricted to the qualified and self-perfecting minorities. The modern tendency is for the mass to ignore these minorities and replace them with themselves in positions of education, politics, art, business, leadership.

The result of this process of the masses assuming "leadership" has been an ironic one, for it has actually resulted in a general rising of the socio-economic and cultural level. In other words, the ordinary standard of living under the masses, Ortega observed, has risen to that possessed only by former minorities. The cause of this rising has been the very real material and social improvements available to all classes and cultures. The historical level of existence, of social and economic well-being, has risen for the average man the world over. But there is an irony and a deception in this well-being, because it has led to a self-satisfaction and inertness that is not warranted.

Because the rise to power of the masses is such a pronounced phenomenon, Ortega believed it is necessary to examine this phenomenon more carefully and deeply. He began with an inquiry into the origin of the masses. He asked how they have been produced and what they are like. Ortega claimed, as Kierkegaard separately perceived, that they are of a nineteenth century origin in both Europe and the Americas. There came into play at that time three different principles that had never existed in combination before: liberal democracy, scientific experiment, and industrialism. Ortega summarized the coming together of these principles in the common expression "technicism." These principles were not all developed in the nineteenth century, but that century implemented them in a new way. Technicism became a revolutionary principle in the nineteenth century, because it enabled the mass to enjoy a new condition of life that was in contradiction to all previous orders. Previously even the rich and powerful found the world a place of difficulty, want, and danger.[11] But the mass production of goods and services in the industrial revolution now suggested even to the common man that a common existence need not be confined to want, that new material and social possibilities existed everywhere. The multitude now found life open in a new way; power and productivity so increased that they came to believe that the worldly possibilities of science and production are a gift of nature, automatic in their bestowal. The common man came to forget that the economic and scientific-industrial facilities always demand the support of definite human competencies and disciplines. Also the new scientific and social organizations placed at their disposal led the masses to believe that their discovery and maintenance were automatic and perfect in the scheme of things, so that the control of circumstances was finally achieved. Ortega summarized his thesis as follows: the perfections of scientific industrialism and liberal democracy caused the masses to believe that their system was not organized and maintained by human excellence, but as a "natural system," free as the air. This has led to a contradictory situation, for the masses are always concerned with their material well-being, but at the same time they remain alien to or ignorant of the causes of that well-being. The level of civilization that they enjoy can be maintained only by effort and excellence. But the masses have come to believe that their authentic role is simply to demand the benefits of the nineteenth and twentieth centuries as though they were natural rights. In this sense the masses remain in contradiction to the conditions which allowed them to come into being.[12] To the masses everything seems now permitted, even demandable, of the new socio-economic system. Everything seems to serve them as a right of consumption, without requirements or duties on the part of the recipients.

While the new average or mass man produced by the nineteenth century was a creature of appetites and demands, he or she also possessed the economic and technical means of satisfying these appetites, at least for the time being. In this seemingly stable condition the mass seemed to find all that was needed in itself; its assumptions about human life were expressed as limitlessness, equality, safety, and self-satisfaction. Such assumptions seemed natural and inevitable, and there seemed no reason for the mass to look outside itself for its perfection. Such assumptions formed the mind of the nineteenth century, a mentality of self-satisfaction and comfort with oneself. Because there was no effective social or economic opposition to these assumptions in the rest of society, the appeal to a higher authority than the mass ceased to exist, and the mass came to believe itself the master of its own existence. But as a master of one's existence one will still remain identical with oneself. One will remain in a self-satisfied state of personal and group inertia.

Ortega contrasted his picture of mass typicality to the "select man," the qualified minority. He distinguished this vital individual as a person who is "urged by an interior necessity" to appeal to a standard superior to him or herself. Such a person accepts this standard of achieving superiority in the spirit of service,[13] continually making higher demands upon himself or herself, and constantly striving to attain something above himself or herself. This minority attempts to transform and absorb circumstances by creating new forms of life.

The mass man, on the other hand, demands only that others be content with him as he is. He refuses to live in servitude to higher standards, or to define himself by obligations. He spends his life in inertia, never attaining surpassing qualities, and always waiting for something outside himself to save or uplift him. The mass seeks to be passively defined and socialized without effort. It tends to assign its existence to some collective, and orient to demanding goals only out of blank necessity. The idea of a self-creating mission is alienating to mass man.[14] This means for Ortega that the mass can enjoy no authentic destiny or vital project in life, and attempts at self-fabrication will be minimal. While the select person will always seek a vocation in concrete life,[15] the mass man possesses no effective "I," but his or her life consists of repeating the normative assumptions of the group; the mass turns itself over to the traditions of its inherited class or background, and avoids any means of self-transcendence.

The upshot of all this, for Ortega as for Nietzsche before him, is that the sense of individual or group mission cannot be expected of the masses, and the highest vocation that can be reasonably assigned to them is the support of what we may call a "vital elite" of those select few whose vocation is to create the goals of humanity. But Ortega also realized that contemporary society is characterized by the fact that the "leadership" of politics, culture, science, art, and literature is so divorced from the vital needs of society that we can no longer rely upon this "leadership" for wisdom. This compounds the contemporary crisis. The role of self-definition has been left to the masses, and for this reason the West is in decline.

The decline of the West is not being counteracted by any adequate personal commitment, and the masses are continuing to live a derivative life of self-satisfaction.[16] To understand better why this is, we must return to Ortega's question of how the mass is born, and look at not only historical but personal development. For Ortega each authentic individual possesses a mission which he or she is called to realize.[17] But the mission of our life is always threatened by the mediation of *alteración*. In this state, we may recall, the human being lives by and within external circumstances, all that is other (*alter*) than the self. Here life ceases to be a personal creation and becomes merely a socialized and external existence. It is altered from its more authentic and original status. We have noted that *alteración* is not necessarily bad or abnormal, for man is required to be concerned with external circumstances if he would survive. But when the individual is captured in the external status, which we have called the masses, the inner, personal, and authentic life is given over and lost; the inner life is no longer a personal creation, and the possibility of a retreat (*ensimismamiento*) into the resources of the self is largely forgotten. The being that is one's own is assigned to the "collectivized other." It is at this point that the mass is born. The autofabrication of one's personal existence is turned over to the thematizing of the "one" as mass.

In order to counteract the decline of the West, the historical construction of human life must be appropriated by those who are capable to autofabricate human life from within. This is the vocation of a select and qualified minority. The select person retains the power of mission, the power to withdraw from the other and take a stand within him or herself. The select person will here follow Pindar's advice to "become what you are," return from the infrahuman mass to a state of *ensimismamiento*, to self-creation from within. In the present state of personal and collective demoralization, there must exist select persons, a vital elite, to perform the mission of self-creation. But such a minority vocation is avoided and resisted by the mass. Because the mass always operates under the assumption that its existence requires no justification, no qualifications of reason or sensibility, it remains identical with itself and refuses internal becoming. The mass limits its self-development to the demand of all rights to all things. It seeks to obtain these even up to the point of dismantling the socio-economic order in which it resides. Because it lacks self-regulation or re-appraisal through the interiority of *ensimismamiento*, the mass also drifts into roles for which it has no vocation or qualifications. It makes decisions and carries out projects, but these lack inner reflection and tend to be guided by the media and contemporary politics. Because the masses are not oriented to the vital requirements of history outside themselves, and because they fail to engage in an authentic vocation, an a-moral or demoralized atmosphere is the result.

Ortega understood our present condition, as did Kierkegaard, Heidegger, and Nietzsche before him, as demoralization or nihilism. For Ortega and Nietzsche, especially, this is the state produced by the lack of standards and qualification, when beliefs have weakened to the extent that those beliefs are inadequate for the conduct of life. Normally society exists on the supposition of effective beliefs and practices, but in demoralization there exists the suspicion that there are no beliefs or actions adequate for dealing with threatening circumstances. It was in the face of this situation that Ortega posed the importance of his qualified minority, which is able to address itself to those historical circumstances that require both *ensimismamiento* and submission to standards above itself. In his *Modern Theme* (1923) Ortega posed the requirement of qualified leadership and interiority for the historical development of the West. He also claimed that the circumstantial crises that require the leadership of a qualified minority are not new. In the middle ages there was the attempt to found qualified leadership in the socio-economic hierarchies of the feudal system. Here the beliefs and the usages of the people were derived from religious and hierarchical sources. In the Renaissance there were posed secular power resolutions to socio-political circumstances. This secular tendency reached its height in the period of the French Revolution with its notions of progress and universal reason as the dominant norms of humanity. In the nineteenth century liberalism, science, and industrialism were considered to be the self-evident criteria for the direction of society. But Ortega, along with Nietzsche, Sorel, and Spengler, came to believe that these criteria have given way to nihilism, massification, and *alteración* in our own century. *The Revolt of the Masses* was Ortega's attempt to proclaim that the survival of the West requires that our present circumstances must now be addressed by the qualified minority for the aborting of demoralization and "the diffuse authoritarianism of the mob."

Ortega saw this mission of the qualified minority as compatible even with classical liberalism. He postulated liberal institutions as a requirement of civilization, and for the effective thinking of circumstances. Liberalism for him referred to the arrangements of constitutional government which provide permanent rights and adequate safeguards against the constraints and conformities of the modern state. He also understood freedom as the self-actualization of those who seek their vocation in the fulfillment of their capacities.[18] Such a vocation must be protected from the impositions of both left and right. This protection is imperative because the "two false dawns" of our century, Bolshevism and Fascism, have both been committed to a *modus operandi* of statism, direct action, and mob violence. The deepest tendency of both movements is to restrict method, reason, and standards. Therefore, the best means of repulsing this tendency to barbarism is liberal constitutionalism, the political principle in which the state limits its authority by respecting the rights and reasonings of those who disagree with it. In this manner it "shares existence" with the enemy. This principle, however, is always at variance with the dispositions of the mass. Also, because liberalism assumes the innate inequality of persons except before the law, there must always be a vigilance in such a polity against any egalitarianism which maintains that equality is more essential to life than freedom. This egalitarianism is itself a mass notion which has always abrogated the claim that effective leadership requires a qualified minority. Indeed, for Ortega civilization requires the division of society into the mass and the qualified minority.

For Ortega the mission of philosophy is always closely related to the above conceptions of freedom and civilization. It is the mission of philosophy to provide the needed clarity and critical analysis, both for the failed beliefs about our life and circumstances and for the new beliefs which can act as alternatives. Philosophy is in fact the creation of the minority for the inquiry into the radical reality of human life. It must decide of human life what it is going to do and be in the future. It is the thinking aspect of the self-creation of human life. But the masses do not understand thinking in this manner. For Ortega the mass is shut up within itself and rests content with the stock of ideas it already possesses. It imagines itself complete and feels no lack of perfection in itself.[19] The mass is open only to prejudices, commonplaces, and idle talk, and it imposes this intellectual vulgarity as a right upon all issues. Prior to the nineteenth century the multitude tended to have no theoretical opinions on politics, literature, or art. Now, said Ortega, the mass believes that it possesses "ideas." But these are not genuine ideas, not genuine culture, for those who seek genuine ideas and culture must submit to the standards and criticisms and authority of agents outside themselves. There can be neither ideas nor culture where standards are absent. All intellectual and scientific issues must in principle be referred to tribunals of some sort. The lack of such qualified agencies Ortega designated as barbarism in a culture. Barbarism is standardlessness. It is the chief characteristic of the masses that they have no wish to submit to any such requirements, and they do not seek them out. In this sense the mass man is an intellectual barbarian. He does not feel it incumbent to give reasons, but only opinions. It is the new fashion, as Ortega said of Europe in 1930, to abandon reason and replace it with action, to impose what a group desires without the mediation of discrimination, judgment, or research.[20] Oddly enough, Ortega included here the present scientist-technician as the very prototype of the mass man. This type emerged around 1890 in the West as a new type of scientist, the specialist. Science itself is not specialism, for if it were, it would cease to be science. The specialist is not learned in the sense demanded of the qualified minority, for he is ignorant of all that does not enter into his specialty. But neither is he entirely ignorant, for he knows his specialty. He should be called "the learned ignoramus," because in all matters outside his field he adopts the attitude of the mass. Specialization has made him hermetic and self-satisfied, and he behaves in most spheres as does the unqualified mass man.

Finally, Ortega saw our greatest enemy as the state, and he was much concerned with the attitude the mass man takes to it. The masses see in the state an anonymous power, and they feel akin to it, because they are themselves anonymous. The mass will not acknowledge that the state is dangerous because it can absorb spontaneous historical action and reflection. It will tend to refer all problems to the state, which seems to promise both safety and satisfaction without extending any requirements upon the individual. The masses believe that they are the state, and they will tend to require that society live for the state. They will demand that the state assume the rights and functions of society, and society will be deemed valuable only to the extent that it lives in the service of the state. The issue of the state is decisive here, because commanding and obeying are central to every society. If this function is in doubt, then all else will be imperfect and ineffective in the social collective. For Ortega commanding and obeying are in doubt today, because both Europe and the Americas have increasingly been left without standards. At the center of our life is the aspiration of the mass to live without standards, and this is the very meaning of the revolt of the masses.

(C) Conclusion

In Ortega's perspective the mass is the possibility of defective human life. It is a social *alteración*, a being-outside oneself in a state of conformity and inertness. Yet for Ortega we cannot define ourselves *solus ipse* as a private world, for we are radically in circumstances, and one of our paramount circumstances is the social other. As in the case of Heidegger we are with others in a world. The other is not merely something contingent or secondary, but a property of how we are and must be in a world. The social other is both useful and dangerous to individual human life. It is useful, because the engagement of circumstances demands of human life concerted social action and cooperation. Culture is impossible without these behaviors. Yet the other is capable of drawing us, and we are capable of drawing ourselves, into an abnormal form of *alteración*, a form of life that has lost the dimension of inner significance and meaning. While it is true for Ortega, as for Heidegger, that we must live by and in everything that surrounds us, everything that is other than ourselves, the other as mass is a defective possibility of our authentic sociality. Here we are not simply with others in society for the negotiation of circumstances, but we have lost sight of our own-most possibilities for being ourselves and creating ourselves. The other is defective when it renders *ensimismamiento* impossible or alienating. In the *alteración* of the masses our inner life is exteriorized and socialized into something that is not our own, but another's. We belong to something outside of ourselves, because we are altered away from a personal mission of self-fabrication, to purposes and values that are outside of ourselves. The mass makes us forget that our true life is to withdraw within ourselves to a more personal and meaningful state. For Ortega, only in *ensimismamiento* is there the authentic possibility of both self-creation and human betterment. To be proscribed or excluded from this inner state and lost in *alteración* is to be wrenched from our historical being, our self-becoming through autofabrication. This autofabrication, our self-becoming, is not something that can be derived from the mass other, but from our inner decision and vocation. The revolt of the masses is the most significant fact of recent times, because it is incompatible with authentic self-creation, because it renders individuation impossible.

For Ortega explicitly, and for Kierkegaard, Nietzsche, and Heidegger implicitly, society is composed of mass and minority. They will use different terms for this division, but the distinction is still within their works. For all of them this distinction is more than a quantitative one; it is more than the declaration that the first category is many and the second few. There exists also a qualitative or normative relation between mass and minority. The implication of Ortega's distinctions in *The Revolt of the Masses* is that our future is threatened in qualitative as well as quantitative terms. While the three other thinkers expressed similar warnings about the quality of man's future, it was Ortega's insight that human life is becoming increasingly unable to orient itself in circumstances, and in this respect human life is becoming de-qualified, due to the inordinate influence of the masses. He has told us in his *Revolt* that even the existence of the masses themselves will become increasingly impossible without a qualified minority; that human life in society is defective to the extent that it is not "aristocratic" or effectively led. The masses, as Nietzsche too proclaimed, increasingly in modern technological circumstances, require, even without their assent, a guiding by a qualified minority. Further, it is the very nature of a viable society to require and form such minorities for group and cultural survival in circumstances. The thrust of Ortega's social thought is to show the necessity for such a vital elite. It is a normalcy of society to require a viable relation between mass and qualified minority. The present decline of a qualified minority, of effective models in government, business, art, religion, literature, philosophy, and education, is abnormal. The present refusal or inability of a minority to fulfill its vital function of leadership and qualification standards has allowed the masses to claim to fulfill a function for which they are constitutionally incapable. Present demoralization, the collective and individual state of life that results from an absence of standards of culture and conduct, has become ever more prominent. The failed beliefs with respect to a meaningful reality have resulted in a current perception of groundlessness for personal and collective life.

As we noted earlier, certain reservations are assumed in this position: the mass-minority dichotomy is not symmetrical with either social class or estates of privilege; it was not Ortega's intention to imply that social stratification is always justified, or always to be defended. He did mean to assert, however, that in all stable societies room must be made for the leadership of a qualified minority. In a healthy collective individuals from any strata must always have access to leadership with the requisite qualifications. Ortega's distinction here is not one between types of men; the great division of individuals is between those who live by standards above themselves and make demands upon themselves, and those who don't; it is between those who are satisfied with themselves as they are as inert and standard-less, and those who seek an existence which is authenticated by the qualified. The mass is barbarian, because it refuses to be judged by the qualified. Yet this issue is even further mediated when Ortega tells us that "the barbarism of specialization" enlists individuals of uncertain qualification into a pseudo elite. Here even the "experts" will feel the need and right to judge and act without authority or qualifications. Here the specialist in one area will not perceive his own limitations and will assume rights and authorities he does not possess in other areas. The expert in accounting will assume an expertise and responsibility in politics and international relations. In sum, the unqualified mass will assume all rights to all things, but without accompanying responsibility or qualifications. In this situation the select minority, for Ortega, must base its claims not on inherited or permanent privilege, but upon the distinctions that arise from self-fabrication. His is the recognition that without the construction of the self under standards of excellence both individuals and society are at risk of inertia and demoralization. For Ortega the mass would nullify this recognition.

Kierkegaard's earlier perspective on the modern crowd was quite unlike that of Ortega's. It was Kierkegaard's mission to have detected the rise of the mass, and to have distinguished it as a philosophical category apart from the "many" or the multitude. In his delineation of the mass he was the first to provide a moral critique of the whole of modernism. Within a year of the publication of Marx's *Communist Manifesto* in 1848 Kierkegaard had written his *Two Ages*; and contrary to the *Manifesto* he proposed that abstract equality is a flawed moral and social norm for both his age and the future. The growth and self-adulation of the crowd was for Kierkegaard but one more suggestion that modernism is fundamentally the substitution of man for God, and such a substitution can only result in moral confusion and unhappiness. Unlike Marx, whom he seems never to have read, Kierkegaard could not accept the problem of the modern age as economic or political, for he could not believe that the derangements of the modern age are simply the result of private property. The source of the leveling and depersonalization of modernism was always seen by Kierkegaard to lie in the individual's abandonment of the eternal, and his attempt to seek salvation in economics, politics, and materialism. These elements were for him also related to the Hegelian tendency of the modern age to deify the state as the culmination of society. The state, more than any other agent, generated the "phantom public," the all-encompassing "something" which is actually nobody. The state appeals to the "phantom public" to act as the hidden agent which supports its engineering and opposes its enemies. In this sense the public appears as a concretized and authoritative agent which embodies the politics and ends of the state itself. Both Ortega and Nietzsche saw the state as a danger that is connected to the rise of the mass.

In Kierkegaard's perspective politics always tends to take on a quasi-religious significance for the crowd, for political goals appear to transcend the merely personal dimension of the individual; yet in everything the crowd attempts to appear in secular dress. It seeks to be understood as the embodiment of "reason." Its idolization of "reason" expresses itself as the search for neutrality and objectivity in all things. But it equally avoids commitment and responsibility. It seeks to relieve collective individuals from the anxiety that freedom and responsibility generate. In such areas as personal guilt and punishment, the crowd tends to reject both factors, because of their suggested critique of the crowd's neutrality and equality or even purely theoretical stance with respect to others. To detect guilt or responsibility is to introduce preferences and inequalities which are unacceptable to the mass. The mass tends to believe that the guilty are in fact morally neutralized by being "victims of societal arrangements." Collective guilt nullifies retribution, and collective innocence is assumed for all non-judicial situations. Good and evil come to be neutralized into a collective indifference. This equality of persons and norms is the very advent of nihilism in the modern era, a nihilism with which modern science cannot deal. In this condition the individual founders. For Kierkegaard his or her situation becomes so desperate that personal rank and value are determined by the ability to endure isolation in the crowd. The mass man, on the other hand, is unable to endure out of the context of the crowd.

In sum, Kierkegaard was the theoretician of the mass from the perspective of egalitarianism and its implications for the authentic destiny of the individual. Kierkegaard's analysis remained apart from considerations of technology, urbanism, economics, or science. His emphasis was the individual first and last. It would remain for the others in this study to fill out his insights in secular areas. Kierkegaard's conclusion was that the individual can overcome the despair and mass leveling of the present age only through the transcendence provided by faith in the eternal; personal existence is finally individuated only in such faith.

Our third perspective upon the mass is that of Friedrich Nietzsche. As the founder of atheistic existentialism Nietzsche proclaimed the death of God and rejected all transmundane salvation. The hope for the human condition he placed in the superman, for the Christian salvational scheme was for him beyond hope or pertinence. He understood our present nihilism as dominant, but transitional. His great philosophical problematic was the advent of nihilism, and he largely understood his mission to be the critique of his era and the transvaluation of nihilistic assumptions by excising their various pathologies. The death of God was for Nietzsche a sort of phenomenological description of the fact that the divine world no longer reveals itself to our condition. God as a supernatural being who provides a source of transcendent truth and value is no longer a useful interpretation of the world. But also for Nietzsche the residue of God's purported existence pervades contemporary life. While the death of God is the assumption of some, the masses, which Nietzsche designated as the "herd" (*Herde*), do not completely realize this event, nor do they understand its implication for existence. The herd's function is both to mask and yet to live out the arrival of nihilism through their translation of Christianity into the themes of equality, progress, democracy, socialism, feminism, and herd values generally. These themes are nihilistic, not only because they transvalue former Christian themes into secular ones, but because they have failed, in Nietzsche's mind, to allow for a viable interpretation of existence.

For Nietzsche the masses and their nihilism are to be understood by a description of their origin and development. One crucial element in this respect is to be found in the phenomenon of resentment (*ressentiment*), the presumption that weakness is a virtue, the attempt of the weak to nullify the superiority of the strong. Nihilism in this context refers to the attempt by the weak to transform the virtues of the strong into the values of the herd, to replace master values with slave values. In this sense the master values become evil and the values of the weak become good. This inversion has become, for Nietzsche, the crucial dimension of herd nihilism, a debasement of life. The genesis of the herd is to be found in this debasement, with equality as its master norm. The herd tends to see its highest worth in its members' likeness of one to another, yet it sanctifies its present status as the highest form of humanity. Only those values that legitimize these assumptions are tolerated, and the herd remains satisfied with its assumption that it represents "the last man," the highest development of humanity. Nietzsche told us through his spokesman Zarathustra that today belongs to the herd, that the herd is the untruth of our condition. The first requirement of life is not to seek truth in the herd. It is the mission of higher humanity, and particularly of Zarathustra, to counteract the herd's present mastery of the earth. The herd must become the servant of the preparation for the superman, the meaning of the earth. The overman became for Nietzsche a metaphor for the guidance of the human race from its present nihilistic status, a metaphor for the need to create a new goal for mankind, which after five thousand years of civilization still has no goal. The preparation for the overman was Nietzsche's response to the nihilism of the herd, yet he knew the herd would continue to refuse such an authentic transcendence, and it would never understand the saving power.

Our one other perspective upon the mass is that of Martin Heidegger. In his thought the mass, the "anybody" self (*das Man*), possesses both a positive and a defective sense. Its positive sense refers to that constitution of the self which is publicly in the world with others. This public world is part of Dasein's own-ness, but it is also shared or "social" in that it governs our interpretation of the public world. Yet there is a defective sense of this anybody self, a sense which is a permanent possibility of Dasein. It is a possibility in which Dasein may participate to various degrees. This defective state is encountered by the self when it goes beyond those uses and expectations required for coping in the public world, and loses responsibility for itself by falling into totalizing conformity with *das Man*. Dasein is defective to the *degree* that it has "fallen" away from its own possibilities, responsibilities, and resoluteness for its own comportment. This defective state is unlike Nietzsche's herd, for Heidegger's *Massenmensch* is more than a collection of post-Christian individuals with nihilistic characteristics. The modern mass for Heidegger is the human being which has understood itself as technological Being. Human Being has become the technological will to power to organize and dominate the earth for economic ends. *Das Man* is here conceived as all humanity subsumed under conformity to the techno-economic will to power. *Das Man* has become conformity to the implicit norm that demands ever higher utilization and consumption of the resources of the earth as a universal right and duty. The falling of the individual into the techno-economic *das Man* is, for Heidegger, the deepest crisis of modernism. This is the nihilism which forms the present posture of mankind.

At this point we have reached the end of our study, though the reader may wish to pursue the topic in other thinkers, such as those mentioned in the Preface. We have identified four significant and representative perspectives upon the mass or crowd in the thought of Kierkegaard, Nietzsche, Heidegger, and Ortega y Gasset. These perspectives must, for the present work at least, constitute the great import of the idea. Yet it would still seem incumbent upon our study to attempt to provide a single sense of the subject which would be symmetrical with all of these perspectives. The following definition is proposed: the mass is the individual when he or she becomes a collective "other" in such a manner that his or her possibilities and concerns are assumed, at least temporarily, by that "other." The cost of this transference is our freedom of self-creation.

Hence it would also seem incumbent on this study to express, in the freedom of self-creation, a personal sense of where humanity stands at the end of the twentieth century, using the perspective of our four thinkers on the Crowd. To this individual it seems that humanity on the whole is still rushing blindly into Ortega's technicism, without heeding its causes or its consequences; into Heidegger's enframed *Gestell*, such that technology is deciding our destiny and exploiting us for stockpiling and the destruction of the earth's resources; into Nietzsche's herd or slave morality, with emphasis on raising standards of living without corresponding demands for leadership or setting higher goals; and into Kierkegaard's leveling, where equality is dictated, not earned, where the media are king, and the vast majority are caught in confusion, alienation, isolation, and despair. Philosophy, which Ortega called to provide a clear analysis both for our failed beliefs and new alternatives, seems instead enslaved by outdated worship of science, reason, and philosophical technology, by the old Cartesian equation of truth with representational abstractions. Yes, the world "hath need" of our four thinkers and of their openness to Being and the auto-fabrication to the future, lest the Crowd be ourselves.

Endnotes

Chapter One

References to the works of Kierkegaard will be abbreviated as follows:

AUC *Kierkegaard's Attack upon "Christendom."* Translated by Walter Lowrie. Princeton: Princeton University Press, 1944.

CA *The Concept of Anxiety* (1844). Translated by Reidar Thomte and Albert B. Anderson. Princeton: Princeton University Press, 1980.

CUP *Concluding Unscientific Postscript.* Translated by David F. Swenson and Walter Lowrie. Princeton: Princeton University Press, 1968.

EO *Either/Or.* Vol. 1. Translated by David F. Swenson, Lillian Marvin Swenson, and Howard A. Johnson. Vol. 2. Translated by Walter Lowrie and Howard A. Johnson. Princeton: Princeton University Press, 1971.

JP *Søren Kierkegaard's Journals and Papers.* Edited and translated by Howard V. Hong and Edna H. Hong. Bloomington: Indiana University Press, 1967-1978.

PF *Philosophical Fragments or a Fragment of Philosophy.* Translated by David F. Swenson and Howard V. Hong. Princeton: Princeton University Press, 1962.

PV *The Point of View for My Work as an Author.* Translated by Walter Lowrie. New York: Harper & Row, 1962.

SUD *The Sickness unto Death.* In *Fear and Trembling and The Sickness unto Death.* Translated by Walter Lowrie. Princeton: Princeton University Press, 1954.

TA *Two Ages. The Age of Revolution and the Present Age.* Edited and translated by Howard V. Hong and Edna H. Hong. Princeton: Princeton University Press, 1978.

1 SUD, 146.

2 Georg Wilhelm Friedrich Hegel, *The Phenomenology of Mind*, translated by J.B. Baillie, (2nd ed.; New York: The Macmillan Company, 1949), pp. 413-453.

3 CUP, 267.

4   CUP, 182.

5   The I-we dialectic has been developed in Merold Westphal, *Kierkegaard's Critique of Reason and Society* (Macon, Georgia: Mercer University Press, 1987), pp. 31-33. The author is indebted to this work.

Chapter Two

1   TA, 84-85.

2   TA, 70.

3   TA, 81.

4   For a discussion of abstract or ethical envy see Robert L. Perkins, "Envy as Personal Phenomenon and as Politics," in *Two Ages: The Present Age and the Age of Revolution, A Literary Review in International Kierkegaard Commentary*, Vol. 14, pp. 107-132. The author is indebted to this work.

5   TA, 88.

6   TA, 84.

7   JP, 4157.

8   TA, 63.

9   JP, 4119.

10 PV, 93-103.

11 PV, 109-120.

12 These theses are developed by Merold Westphal, *op. cit.*, p. 34.

Chapter Three

1   Heidegger would describe his early education and such early influences on his life in a late essay entitled "My Way to Phenomenology." This appears in a collection of essays entitled *On Time and Being*, edited and translated by Joan Stambaugh (New York: Harper & Row, 1972), pp. 74-82.

2   *Sein und Zeit*, pp. 27-39; hereafter cited as SZ and page number. My references are to the seventh edition of *Sein und Zeit* (1953) published by Max Niemeyer Verlag, Tübingen, 1979. These German pages appear cited in the margin of the English edition of *Being and Time* (New York: Harper & Row, 1962), translated by John Macquarrie and Edward Robinson. I will cite the German first.

3 William J. Richardson, *Heidegger Through Phenomenology to Thought* (2nd ed.; The Hague: Martinus Nijhoff, 1967), p. xiv. See also Martin Heidegger, *Platons Lehre von der Wahrheit. Mit einem Brief über den Humanismus* (Bern: A. Franke, 1947). Translated by Edgar Lohner as "Letter on Humanism" in *Philosophy in the Twentieth Century*, ed. William Barrett and Henry Aiken (New York: Random House, 1962), Vol. III, p. 287.

4 Martin Heidegger, *Identität und Differenz* (Pfullingen: Neske, 1957), p. 66. Translated as *Identity and Difference* by Joan Stambaugh (New York: Harper & Row, 1969), p. 62.

5 SZ, 153 (195 English translation).

6 SZ, 344 (394).

7 SZ, 114 (150).

8 SZ, 167 (210).

9 SZ, 192 (237).

10 SZ, 130 (168).

11 SZ, 118 (154).

12 SZ, 288 (334).

13 SZ, 130 (168).

14 SZ, 127 (165).

15 SZ, 113-130 (149-168).

16 SZ, 127 (164).

17 SZ, 128 (165).

18 SZ, 127 (165).

19 SZ, 128 (165).

20 SZ, 175 (220).

21 SZ, 178 (222).

22 SZ, 318 (354).

23 SZ, 383 (435).

24 The themes of technological modernism and of the authentic self in Heidegger are developed in Michael Zimmerman's *Eclipse of the Self. The Development of Heidegger's Concept of Authenticity* (Athens: Ohio

University Press, 1981), especially pp. 218-228. Also see his *Heidegger's Confrontation with Modernity. Technology, Politics, Art* (Bloomington: Indiana University Press, 1990), especially Chapters 3, 4, 5, 10, 11, and 13, pp. 205-221. The author is indebted to both of these works.

25 SZ, 375 (427).

26 SZ, 347 (398).

27 SZ, 387 (439).

28 SZ, 391 (443).

29 Kierkegaard, CUP, p. 119. Herbert Marcuse also makes this claim in his analysis of Hegel. Cf. Herbert Marcuse, *Hegel's Ontology and the Theory of Historicality*, translated by Seyta Benhabib (Cambridge: MIT Press, 1987), p. 2.

Chapter Four

1 The author is indebted to William Lawhead's unpublished manuscript entitled "The Voyage of Discovery. A History of Western Philosophy," Chapter 27: "Friedrich Nietzsche," especially for its biographical and perspectivism sections.

2 Friedrich Nietzsche, *The Will to Power*, translated by Walter Kaufmann and R.J. Hollingdale (New York: Vintage Books, 1968), section 259. Abbreviated as WP.

3 WP, 1067.

4 WP, 552.

5 WP, 280.

6 WP, 993.

7 WP, 284.

8 WP, 69.

9 WP, 7.

10 WP, 276-278.

11 WP, 684.

12 WP, 12-13.

13 WP, 972-993.

14 Martin Heidegger, *Nietzsche*, Vol. IV (Nihilism), translated by Frank A. Capuzzi and David F. Krell (New York: Harper & Row, 1982), p. 46.

15 *Ibid.*, p. 216.

16 *Ibid.*, p. 52.

17 *Ibid.*, p. 218.

18 *Ibid.*, p. 229.

19 *Ibid.*, p. 248.

20 *Ibid.*, p. 552.

21 The distinction between "conformity" and "conformism" with respect to our own-ness as Being-in-the-world has been developed in his excellent commentary on *Being and Time*. See Hubert L. Dreyfus, *Being-in-the-World. A Commentary on Heidegger's Being and Time, Division I* (Cambridge: MIT Press, 1991), pp. 154-162. The author is indebted to this work's distinction of terms here.

22 Martin Heidegger, "The Question Concerning Technology" in *The Question Concerning Technology and Other Essays*, translated by William Lovitt (New York: Harper & Row, 1977), p. 4.

23 Heidegger, "The Age of the World Picture" in *The Question Concerning Technology and Other Essays*, pp. 115-154.

24 See Ernst Jünger, *Der Arbeiter* (Hamburg: Hanseatische Verlagsanstalt, 1932).

25 SZ, 117 (153).

26 SZ, 130 (168).

27 This thesis is developed in Hubert L. Dreyfus and Jane Rubin, "Kierkegaard, Division II, and Later Heidegger" in Dreyfus, *op. cit.*, pp. 283-340. The author is indebted to this work.

28 SZ, 178 (223).

Chapter Five

1 *Obras completas*, Vol. 7, p. 369. All references to the works of Ortega y Gasset are from his *Obras completas*, 1st edition, 12 volumes (Madrid: Alianza-Revista de Occidente, 1983). Subsequent citations will use the form *Obras* with volume number, then page number, e.g., *Obras* 7, 369.

2 *Obras* 8, 311.

3   The author is indebted to the biographical section of Victor Ouimette, *José Ortega y Gasset* (Boston: Twayne Publishers, 1982), pp. 15-36.

4   For an explanation and critical analysis of the relation of Ortega to the thought of Dilthey and Heidegger, see the author's *The Dawn of Historical Reason. The Historicality of Human Existence in the Thought of Dilthey, Heidegger, and Ortega y Gasset* (New York: Peter Lang, 1994).

5   According to his disciple Julián Marías, Ortega had achieved the idea of human life as radical reality as early as 1914-1916, especially in his *Meditations on Quixote*. See Julián Marías, *José Ortega y Gasset. Circumstances and Vocation*, translated by F.M. López-Morillas (Norman: University of Oklahoma Press, 1970), p. 433.

6   *Obras* 8, 273.

7   *Obras* 7, 100.

8   *Obras* 7, 275-438. Translated by Mildred Adams as *What Is Philosophy?* (New York: W.W. Norton, 1964).

9   The issue of Being is raised in many places. See, for example, his "Pure Philosophy" (*Obras* 4, 48-59); *Some Lessons in Metaphysics* (*Obras* 8, 270-292); also *Obras* 12, 26-38, 97-101.

10   *Obras* 8, 270-292; 7, 36-37, 103-105.

11   *Obras* 5, 40.

12   *Obras* 6, 46.

13   *Obras* 7, 117.

14   *Obras* 5, 37.

15   *Obras* 9, 396-398.

16   *Obras* 6, 49-50.

17   *Obras* 6, 41.

18   *Obras* 6, 49.

19   *Obras* 6, 49.

Chapter Six

1   *Obras* 7, 124-125.

2   José Ortega y Gasset, *Man and People*, translated by Willard R. Trask (New York: W.W. Norton, 1957), pp. 38ff., 57ff., 72ff.

3 *Obras* 7, 198-200.

4 *Obras* 7, 199.

5 *Obras* 7, 207-208.

6 *Obras* 5, 295-315. This essay is also found in English in *Man and People* (cited above), pp. 11-37.

7 *Obras* 7, 83.

8 *Obras* 7, 88.

9 *Obras* 4, 143.

10 *Obras* 4, 145-146.

11 *Obras* 4, 177.

12 *Obras* 4, 179.

13 *Obras* 4, 182-183.

14 *Obras* 5, 209ff.

15 *Obras* 5, 171.

16 *Obras* 3, 152.

17 *Obras* 5, 209.

18 *Obras* 4, 221.

19 *Obras* 4, 186-187.

20 *Obras* 4, 190.

Bibliography

●

Kierkegaard: Selected Bibliography

I English Translations of Kierkegaard's Writings

Kierkegaard's Attack upon "Christendom." Translated by Walter Lowrie. Princeton: Princeton University Press, 1944.

The Concept of Anxiety (1844). Translated by Reidar Thomte and Albert B. Anderson. Princeton: Princeton University Press, 1980.

Concluding Unscientific Postscript. Translated by David F. Swenson and Walter Lowrie. Princeton: Princeton University Press, 1968.

Either/Or. Vol. I. Translated by David F. Swenson, Lillian Marvin Swenson, and Howard A. Johnson. Vol. II. Translated by Walter Lowrie and Howard A. Johnson. Princeton: Princeton University Press, 1971.

Fear and Trembling and The Sickness unto Death. Translated by Walter Lowrie. Princeton: Princeton University Press, 1954.

Søren Kierkegaard's Journals and Papers. Edited and translated by Howard V. Hong and Edna H. Hong. 7 Vols. Bloomington: Indiana University Press, 1967-1978.

Philosophical Fragments or a Fragment of Philosophy. Translated by David F. Swenson. Princeton: Princeton University Press, 1980.

The Point of View for My Work as an Author, including "The Individual: Two Notes Concerning My Work as an Author" and "My Activity as a Writer." Translated by Walter Lowrie. New York: Harper & Row, 1962.

Two Ages. The Age of Revolution and the Present Age. A Literary Review (1846). Edited and translated by Howard V. Hong and Edna H. Hong. Princeton: Princeton University Press, 1978.

II Selected Secondary Works

Collins, James. *The Mind of Kierkegaard*. Princeton: Princeton University Press, 1983.

Connell, George B. and Evans, C. Stephen, eds. *Foundations of Kierkegaard's Vision of Community*. Atlantic Highlands, N.J.: Humanities Press, 1992.

Dietrichson, Paul. "Kierkegaard's Concept of the Self." *Inquiry* 8 (Spring 1965): 1-32.

Drucker, Peter. "Unfashionable Kierkegaard." *Sewanee Review* 57 (October 1949): 587-602.

Dupré, Louis K. "The Constitution of the Self in Kierkegaard's Philosophy." *International Philosophical Quarterly* 3 (December 1963): 506-526.

Fletcher, David Bruce. *Social and Political Perspectives on the Thought of Søren Kierkegaard*. Washington, D.C.: University Press of America, 1982.

Hegel, G.W.F. *The Phenomenology of Mind*. Translated by J.B. Baillie. 2nd ed. New York: The MacMillan Company, 1949.

Hubben, William. *Dostoevsky, Kierkegaard, Nietzsche, and Kafka. Four Prophets of Our Destiny*. New York: Collier, 1962.

Janik, Allan. "Haecker, Kierkegaard and the Early Brenner: A Contribution to the History of the Reception of *Two Ages* in the German-speaking World." *International Kierkegaard Commentary* 14. Macon, Georgia: Mercer University Press, 1984.

Lawson, Lewis A., ed. *Kierkegaard's Presence in Contemporary American Life*. Metuchen, N.J.: The Scarecrow Press, 1970.

Levi, Albert W. "The Idea of Socrates: The Philosophic Hero in the Nineteenth Century." *Journal of the History of Ideas* 17 (January 1956): 89-108.

Löwith, Karl. *From Hegel to Nietzsche*. Translated by David D. Green. New York: Holt, Rinehart & Winston, 1964.

Lowrie, Walter. *Kierkegaard*. 2 Vols. New York: Harper & Row, 1962.

Lukàcs, György. *The Destruction of Reason*. Translated by Peter Palmer. Atlantic Highlands, N.J.: Humanities Press, 1980.

Lund, Margaret. "The Single Ones." *Personalist* 41 (Winter 1960): 15-24.

Mackey, Louis. "The Loss of the World in Kierkegaard's Ethics." *Kierkegaard. A Collection of Critical Essays*. Edited by Josiah Thompson. New York: Doubleday, 1972.

Magurshak, Daniel. "The Concept of Anxiety: The Keystone of the Kierkegaard-Heidegger Relationship." *International Kierkegaard Commentary* 8. Macon, Georgia: Mercer University Press, 1984.

Malantschuk, Gregor. *The Controversial Kierkegaard*. Translated by Howard V. Hong and Edna H. Hong. Waterloo, Ontario: Wilfrid Laurier Press, 1980.

———. *Kierkegaard's Thought*. Edited and translated by Howard V. Hong and Edna H. Hong. Princeton: Princeton University Press, 1974.

Marcel, Gabriel. *Man Against Mass Society*. Chicago: Henry Regnery, 1952.

Mullen, John Douglas. *Kierkegaard's Philosophy. Self-Deception and Cowardice in the Present Age*. New York: New American Library, 1981.

Niebuhr, H. Richard. *Christ and Culture*. New York: Harper & Row, 1951.

Perkins, Robert L., ed. *The Corsair Affair. International Kierkegaard Commentary*. Macon, Georgia: Mercer University Press, 1990.

———. "Envy as Personal Phenomenon and as Politics" in *Two Ages: The Present Age and the Age of Revolution. A Literary Review. International Kierkegaard Commentary* 14. Macon, Georgia: Mercer University Press, 1984.

———. *Søren Kierkegaard*. Atlanta: John Knox Press, 1969.

———. ed. *Two Ages: The Present Age and the Age of Revolution. A Literary Review. International Kierkegaard Commentary* 14. Macon, Georgia: Mercer University Press, 1984.

Schact, Richard. *Hegel and After*. Pittsburgh: University of Pittsburgh Press, 1975.

Sontag, Frederick. "Kierkegaard and the Search for a Self." *Journal of Existentialism* 7 (Summer 1967): 443-457.

Stack, George J. "Concern in Kierkegaard and Heidegger." *Philosophy Today* 12 (1969): 26-35.

Stark, Werner. "Kierkegaard on Capitalism." *Sociological Review* 42, no. 5 (1950): 87-114.

———. *Social Theory and Christian Thought*. London: Routledge & Kegan Paul, 1959.

Stern, Guenther. "On the Pseudo-Concreteness of Heidegger's Philosophy." *Philosophy and Phenomenological Research* 8 (March 1948): 337-370.

Swenson, David F. "The Anti-Intellectualism of Kierkegaard." *Kierkegaard's Presence in Contemporary American Life*. Metuchen, N.J.: The Scarecrow Press, 1970.

———. "A Danish Thinker's Estimate of Journalism." *International Journal of Ethics* 38 (October 1927): 70-87.

Taylor, Mark. *Journeys to Selfhood: Hegel and Kierkegaard*. Berkeley: University of California Press, 1980.

Thompson, Josiah, ed. *Kierkegaard: A Collection of Critical Essays*. Garden City: Anchor Books, 1972.

Westphal, Merold. *Kierkegaard's Critique of Reason and Society*. Macon, Georgia: Mercer University Press, 1987.

——. "Kierkegaard's Politics." *Thought* 55, no. 218 (1980): 320-332.

Wyschogrod, M. *Kierkegaard and Heidegger*. New York: Humanities Press, 1954.

Nietzsche: Selected Bibliography

I Nietzsche's Bibliography

For Nietzsche's original works see *Werke: Kritische Gesamtausgabe*. Edited by Georgio Colli and Mazzino Montmari. 30 vols. Berlin: de Gruyter, 1967-1978. For an English bibliography see Aleander Nehamas, *Nietzsche. Life as Literature*. Cambridge: Harvard University Press, 1985.

II English Translations of Nietzsche's Writings

Beyond Good and Evil. Translated by Walter Kaufmann. New York: Vintage Books, 1966.

On the Genealogy of Morals. Translated by Walter Kaufmann and R.J. Hollingdale in *On the Genealogy of Morals and Ecce Homo*. Edited by Walter Kaufmann. New York: Vintage Books, 1969.

Thus Spoke Zarathustra in *The Portable Nietzsche* (cited below).

Twilight of the Idols in *The Portable Nietzsche*.

The Will to Power. Translated by Walter Kaufmann and R.J. Hollingdale. New York: Vintage Books, 1968.

The Portable Nietzsche. Translated and edited by Walter Kaufmann. New York: Viking Press, 1968.

III Selected Secondary Sources on Nietzsche

Bergmann, Peter. *Nietzsche: The Last Anti-Political German*. Bloomington: Indiana University Press, 1987.

Copleston, Frederick. *Friedrich Nietzsche: Philosopher of Culture*. London: Burns, Oakes & Washburn, 1942.

Detwiler, Bruce. *Nietzsche and the Politics of Aristocratic Radicalism*. Chicago: University of Chicago Press, 1990.

Heller, Erich. *The Importance of Nietzsche*. Chicago: University of Chicago Press, 1988.

Hollingdale, R.J. *Nietzsche: The Man and His Philosophy*. Baton Rouge: Louisiana State University Press, 1965.

Nehamas, Aleander. *Nietzsche. Life as Literature*. Cambridge: Harvard University Press, 1985.

Scheler, Max. *Ressentiment*. Translated by Lewis Coser. New York: Free Press, 1961.

Strong, Tracy B. *Friedrich Nietzsche and the Politics of Transfiguration*. Berkeley: University of California Press, 1975.

Heidegger: Selected Bibliography

I Heidegger's Bibliography

For a general bibliography see Hans-Martin Sass, *Martin Heidegger: Bibliography and Glossary*. Bowling Green, Ohio: Philosophy Documentation Center, Bowling Green State University, 1982. A Bibliographical Guide is in Michael Murray, ed., *Heidegger and Modern Philosophy: Critical Essays*. New Haven: Yale University Press, 1978, pp. 355-365. Heidegger's complete works are presently being published in the *Gesamtausgabe* by Klostermann in Frankfurt, 1972 to the present (1995 and beyond).

II Selected Works of Heidegger with Current English Translations

Die Grundprobleme der Phänomenologie (1927). Frankfurt: Klostermann, 1975. Translated by Albert Hofstadter as *The Basic Problems of Phenomenology*. Bloomington: Indiana University Press, 1982.

Einführung in die Metaphysik (1935). Tübingen: Niemeyer, 1953. Translated by Ralph Manheim as *An Introduction to Metaphysics*. New Haven: Yale University Press, 1959.

Gelassenheit (1959). Pfullingen: Neske, 1959. Translated by John M. Anderson and E. Hans Freund as *Discourse on Thinking*. New York: Harper & Row, 1966.

Nietzsche (1931-1946). 2 vols. Pfullingen: Neske, 1961.

Nietzsche. Vol.I: *The Will to Power as Art*. Translated by David Farrell Krell. New York: Harper & Row, 1979.

Nietzsche. Vol. II: *The Eternal Recurrence of the Same*. Translated by David Farrell Krell. New York: Harper & Row, 1982.

Nietzsche. Vol. III: *The Will to Power as Knowledge and as Metaphysics*. Translated by Joan Stambaugh, David Farrell Krell, and Frank A. Capuzzi. New York: Harper & Row, 1987.

Nietzsche. Vol. IV: *Nihilism*. Translated by Frank A. Capuzzi and David Farrell Krell. New York: Harper & Row, 1982.

Prolegomena zur Geschichte des Zeitbegriffs (1925). Edited by Petra Joeger. Frankfurt: Klostermann, 1979. Translated by Theodore Kisiel as *History of the Concept of Time*. Bloomington: Indiana University Press, 1992.

"Science and Reflection." In *Martin Heidegger, The Question Concerning Technology and Other Essays*. Translated by William Lovitt. New York: Harper & Row, 1977.

Sein und Zeit (1927). Tübingen: Niemeyer, 1927. Translated by John Macquarrie and Edward Robinson as *Being and Time.* New York: Harper & Row, 1962. With marginal pagination of the German edition of *Sein und Zeit* (7th ed.).

"The Age of the World Picture." In *Martin Heidegger, The Question Concerning Technology and Other Essays.* Translated by William Lovitt. New York: Harper & Row, 1977.

Vorträge und Aufsätze (1936-53). Pfullingen: Neske, 1954. This is a collection of eleven essays which includes the following English translation: "The Question Concerning Technology." In *Martin Heidegger, The Question Concerning Technology and Other Essays.* Translated by William Lovitt. New York: Harper & Row, 1977.

III Selected Secondary Sources

Alderman, Harold. "Heidegger's Critique of Science and Technology." *Heidegger and Modern Philosophy.* Edited by Michael Murray. New Haven: Yale University Press, 1978.

Barash, Jeffrey A. *Martin Heidegger and the Problem of Historical Meaning.* Dordrecht: Martinus Nijhoff, 1988.

Biddis, Michael O. *The Age of the Masses.* New York: Harper & Row, 1977.

Blitz, Mark. *Heidegger's Being and Time and the Possibility of Political Philosophy.* Ithaca: Cornell University Press, 1982.

Camele, Anthony. "Heideggerian Ethics." *Philosophy Today* 21 (1977): 284-293.

Caputo, John D. "Heidegger's Original Ethics." *The New Scholasticism* 45 (1971): 127-138.

Dreyfus, Hubert L. *Being-in-the-World. A Commentary on Heidegger's Being and Time, Division I.* Cambridge: MIT Press, 1991.

Dreyfus, Hubert L. and Zimmerman, Michael, eds. *Applied Heidegger*. Evanston: Northwestern University Press, 1991.

Driscoll, Giles. "Heidegger: A Response to Nihilism." *Philosophy Today* 2 (1967): 17-37.

——. "Heidegger's Ethical Monism." *The New Scholasticism* 42 (1968): 497-510.

Freund, E.H. "Man's Fall in Martin Heidegger's Philosophy." *Journal of Religion* 24 (1944): 180-187.

Giner, Salvador. *Mass Society*. New York: Academic Press, 1976.

Habermas, Jürgen. "Work and Weltanschauung: The Heidegger Controversy from a German Perspective." *The New Conservatism. Cultural Criticism and the Historian's Debate*. Cambridge: MIT Press, 1990.

Hoy, David C. "History, Historicality, and Historiography in *Being and Time*." *Heidegger and Modern Philosophy*. New Haven: Yale University Press, 1978.

Jünger, Ernst. *Der Arbeiter*. Hamburg: Hanseatische Verlagsanstalt, 1932.

Kockelmans, Joseph, ed. *Heidegger and Science. Current Continental Research*. Boston: University Press of America, 1985.

Löwith, Karl. *Heidegger: Denker in dürftiger Zeit*. 2nd ed. Göttingen: Vandenhoek und Ruprecht, 1960.

Magnus, Bernd. *Heidegger's Metahistory of Philosophy: Amor Fati, Being and Truth*. The Hague: Martinus Nijhoff, 1971.

Marcuse, Herbert. "Über konkrete Philosophie." *Archiv für Sozialwissenschaft und Sozialpolitik* 62 (1929): 111-128.

Maurer, Reinhart. "From Heidegger to Practical Philosophy." Translated by Walter E. Wright. *Idealistic Studies* 3 (May 1973): 133-162.

Murray, Michael, ed. *Heidegger and Modern Philosophy*. New Haven: Yale University Press, 1978.

O'Meara, Thomas F. "Tillich and Heidegger: A Structural Relationship." *Harvard Theological Review* 61 (1969): 249-261.

Peccone, Paul and Delfin, Aleander. "Herbert Marcuse's Heideggerean Marxism." *Telos* (Fall 1970): 36-46.

Perotti, James L. *Heidegger and the Divine*. Athens: Ohio University Press, 1974.

Pöggeler, Otto. "Heidegger Today." *Martin Heidegger in Europe and America*. Edited by E.G. Ballard and C.E. Scott. The Hague: Martinus Nijhoff, 1973.

———. *Martin Heidegger's Path of Thinking*. Translated by Daniel Magurshak and Sigmund Barber. Atlantic Highlands, N.J.: Humanities Press, 1987.

Richardson, William J. *Heidegger. Through Phenomenology to Thought*. 2nd ed. The Hague: Martinus Nijhoff, 1967.

Rollin, Bernard. "Heidegger's Philosophy of History in Being and Time." *Modern Schoolman* 49 (January 1972): 97-112.

Schürmann, Reiner. "Anti-Humanism: Reflections of the Turn Toward the Post Modern Epoch." *Man and World* 12, no. 2 (1979): 160-177.

Solomon, Robert C. *Continental Philosophy Since 1750. The Rise and Fall of the Self*. Oxford: Oxford University Press, 1988.

Tuttle, Howard N. *The Dawn of Historical Reason. The Historicality of Human Existence in the Thought of Dilthey, Heidegger, and Ortega y Gasset*. New York: Peter Lang, 1994.

Wren, Thomas E. "Heidegger's Philosophy of History." *Journal of the British Society for Phenomenology* 9 (May 1978): 126-130.

Wyschogrod, M. *Kierkegaard and Heidegger. Ontology of Existence*. London: Routledge & Kegan Paul, 1954.

Zimmerman, Michael. "A Comparison of Marx and Heidegger on the Technological Domination of Nature." *Philosophy Today* 23 (Summer 1979): 99-112.

——. "A Comparison of Nietzsche's Overman and Heidegger's Authentic Self." *Journal of Philosophy* 14 (Spring 1976): 213-231.

——. *Eclipse of the Self. The Development of Heidegger's Concept of Authenticity*. Athens: Ohio University Press, 1986.

——. "Heidegger and Bultmann: Egoism, Sinfulness and Inauthenticity." *Modern Schoolman* 57 (November 1980): 1-20.

——. "Heidegger and Marcuse: Technology as Ideology." *Research in Philosophy and Technology*. Vol. 2. Edited by Paul T. Durbin and Carl Mitcham. Greenwich, Conn.: Jai Press, 1979.

——. *Heidegger's Confrontation with Modernity. Technology, Politics, Art*. Bloomington: Indiana University Press, 1990.

Ortega y Gasset: Selected Bibliography

I General Bibliography

Antón Donoso and Harold Raley have published a general bibliography of secondary sources entitled *José Ortega y Gasset: A Bibliography of Secondary Sources*. Bowling Green, Ohio: Bowling Green State University, Philosophy Documentation Center, 1986. It contains over 4000 entries and includes books, essays, journal and newspaper articles, encyclopedia entries, dissertations, recordings, and films. It also has an extensive subject index. 449 pages. The complete works of Ortega in Spanish are published as

Obras completas. 4th ed. Vols. 1-6. Madrid: Revista de Occidente, 1957.

Obras completas. 3rd ed. Vol. 7. Madrid: Revista de Occidente, 1969.

Obras completas. 2nd ed. Vols. 8-9. Madrid: Revista de Occidente, 1965.

Obras completas. 1st ed. Vols. 10-11. Madrid: Revista de Occidente, 1969.

Obras completas. 1st ed. 12 Vols. Madrid: Alianza Editorial-Revista de Occidente, 1983.

Epistolario. Edited and introduced by Paulino Garagorri. Madrid: Revista de Occidente, 1974.

II Ortega's Selected Works in English

Concord and Liberty. Translated by Helene Weyl. New York: W.W. Norton, 1946.

The Dehumanization of Art and Other Essays on Art, Culture and Literature. Translated by Helene Weyl et al. Princeton: Princeton University Press, 1968.

Historical Reason. Translated by Philip W. Silver. New York: W.W. Norton, 1984.

History as a System. Translated by Helene Weyl and William C. Atkinson. New York: W.W. Norton, 1941.

The Idea of Principle in Leibniz and the Evolution of Deductive Theory. Translated by Mildred Adams. New York: W.W. Norton, 1971.

An Interpretation of Universal History. Translated by Mildred Adams. New York: W.W. Norton, 1973.

Invertebrate Spain. Translated by Mildred Adams. New York: Howard Fertig, 1974.

Man and Crisis. Translated by Mildred Adams. New York: W.W. Norton, 1958.

Man and People. Translated by Willard B. Trask. New York: W.W. Norton, 1957.

Meditations on Hunting. Translated by Howard B. Wescott. New York: Scribner's, 1985.

Meditations on Quixote. Translated by Evelyn Rugg and Diego Marín. Introduction by Julián Marías. New York: W.W. Norton, 1961.

Mission of the University. Translated by Howard Lee Nostrand. New York: W.W. Norton, 1966.

The Modern Theme. Translated by James Cleugh. New York: W.W. Norton, 1933.

On Love: Aspects of a Single Theme. Translated by Toby Talbot. Cleveland: World Publishing, 1957.

The Origin of Philosophy. Translated by Toby Talbot. New York: W.W. Norton, 1967.

Phenomenology and Art. Translated and with an introduction by Philip W. Silver. New York: W.W. Norton, 1975.

Psychological Investigations. Translated by Jorge García-Gómez. New York: W.W. Norton, 1987.

The Revolt of the Masses. 25th anniversary ed. Translator anonymous. New York: W.W. Norton, 1957.

Some Lessons in Metaphysics. Translated by Mildred Adams. New York: W.W. Norton, 1969.

What is Philosophy? Translated by Mildred Adams. New York: W.W. Norton, 1960.

III Selected Secondary Sources

Acuna, Hernan Larrain. *La Genesis del Pensamiento de Ortega.* Buenos Aires: Compania General Fabril, 1962.

Adams, Mildred. "Ortega y Gasset." *Forum and Century* 90 (July-December 1933): 373-378.

Alluntis, Felix. "Radical Reality According to Don José Ortega y Gasset." In John Ryan, ed., *Studies in Philosophy and the History of Philosophy*. Washington: Catholic University of America Press, 1969.

——. "The Vital and Historical Reason of Ortega y Gasset." *Franciscan Studies* 15, no. 1 (1955): 60-78.

Aranguren, José. *La ética de Ortega*. 2nd ed. Madrid: Taurus Ediciones, 1959.

Armstrong, A. "The Philosophy of Ortega y Gasset." *Philosophical Quarterly* 2, no. 7 (1952): 124-138.

Artola, Miguel. "En torno al concepto de historia." *Revista de estudios politicos* 62, no. 99 (1958): 145-183.

Bareo, Arturo. "The Conservative Critics: Ortega and Madariaga." *University Observer* 1 (Winter 1947): 29-36.

Basdekis, Demetrios. *The Evolution of Ortega y Gasset as Literary Critic*. Lanham, MD: University Press of America, 1986.

Benítez, Jaime. *Political and Philosophical Theories of José Ortega y Gasset*. Chicago: University of Chicago Press, 1939.

Borel, Jean-Paul. *Introduccíon a Ortega y Gasset*. Translated by Laureano Perez Latorre. Madrid: Ediciones Guadarrama, 1969.

Ceplecha, Christian. *The Historical Thought of José Ortega y Gasset*. Washington: Catholic University of America Press, 1958.

Curtius, Ernst R. "Ortega." *Partisan Review* 17 (March 1950): 259-271.

De Kalb, Courtenay. "The Spiritual Law of Gravitation: Minority Rule as Analyzed by Ortega." *Hispania* 14 (March 1931): 81-88.

De Puy, Ida B. *The Basic Ideology of José Ortega y Gasset: The Conflict of Mission and Vocation.* Palo Alto: Stanford University Microfilms, 1961.

Díaz, Janet W. *The Major Themes of Existentialism in the Work of José Ortega y Gasset.* Chapel Hill: University of North Carolina Press, 1970.

Donoso, Antón. "The Influence of José Ortega y Gasset in Latin America." *Filosofía* (Sao Paolo) 3 (1974): 43-49.

——. "Society as Aristocratic. Towards a Clarification of the Meaning of Society in Ortega's *The Revolt of the Masses.*" *Analecta Husserliana* 26.

Duran, Manuel. "Tres Definidores del Hombre-Masa: Heidegger, Ortega, Riesman." *Cuadernos Americanos* 90, no. 6 (1956): 115-129.

Fernández, Pelayo H., et al., ed. *Ortega y Gasset Centennial/ University of New Mexico.* Madrid: José Porrua Turanzas, 1985.

Ferrater Mora, José. *Ortega y Gasset: An Outline of His Philosophy.* New rev. ed., New Haven: Yale University Press, 1963.

——. *Studies in Modern European Literature and Thought.* New Haven: Yale University Press, 1957.

Gaete, Arturo. *El sistema de Ortega.* Buenos Aires: Compania General Fabril, 1962.

Gaos, José. *Sobre Ortega y Gasset.* Mexico City: Imprenta Universitaria, 1957.

Garcia, Astrada A. "Filosofía social y sociología in Ortega y Gasset." *Humanities,* Ano VII, no. 11 (1959): 79-90.

Giner, Salvador. *Mass Society.* New York: Academic Press, 1976.

Goyenechea, Francisco. "Lo individual y lo social en la filosofía de Ortega y Gasset." Zürich: *Studia Philosophica* 2 (1964).

Gray, Rockwell. *The Imperative of Modernity. An Intellectual Biography of José Ortega y Gasset.* Berkeley: University of California Press, 1989.

Guy, Alain. *Ortega y Gasset, ou la Raison Vital et Historique.* Paris Editions Seghers, 1969.

Heidegger, Martin. "Encuentros con Ortega y Gasset en Alemania." *Clavileno* 7, no. 39 (1956): 1-2.

Hempel, Carl. "The Function of General Laws in History." In Patrick Gardiner, ed., *Theories of History.* Glencoe: The Free Press, 1963, pp. 344-356.

Holmes, Oliver W. *Human Reality and the Social World: Ortega's Philosophy of History.* Amherst: University of Massachusetts Press, 1975.

Kern, Robert W. *Liberals, Reformers and Caciques in Restoration Spain, 1875-1909.* Albuquerque: University of New Mexico Press, 1975.

Klibansky, Raymond and Paton, H.J., eds. *Philosophy and History. Essays Presented to Ernst Cassirer.* Oxford: Clarendon Press, 1936.

López-Morillas, Juan. "Ortega y Gasset: Historicism vs. Classicism." *Yale French Studies* 6 (1950): 63-74.

Maldonado-Denis, Manuel. "Ortega y Gasset and the Theory of the Masses." *Western Political Quarterly* 14 (September-December 1961): 676-690.

Marías, Julián. *Generations: A Historical Method.* Translated by Harold C. Raley. University: University of Alabama Press, 1970.

———. *History of Philosophy.* Translated by Stanley Appelbaum and C.C. Strowbridge. New York: Dover Publications, 1967, pp. 442-462.

——. *José Ortega y Gasset. Circumstances and Vocation.* Translated by F.M. López-Morillas. Norman: University of Oklahoma Press, 1970.

——. *La Escuela de Madrid: Estudios de Filosofía Espanola.* Buenos Aires: Emece, 1959.

——. *Metaphysical Anthropology: The Empirical Structure of Human Life.* Translated by Frances López-Morillas. University Park: Pennsylvania State University Press, 1971.

Martinez, M. "The Historical Relativism of Ortega y Gasset." *American Catholic Philosophical Association* (1947): 193-211.

Mattei, Carlos Ramos. *Ethical Self-Determination in Ortega y Gasset.* New York: Peter Lang, 1987.

McClintock, Robert. *Man and His Circumstances: Ortega as Educator.* New York: Columbia University Teacher's College Press, 1971.

Morón Arroyo, Ciriaco. *El sistema de Ortega y Gasset.* Madrid: Alcalá, 1968.

Nicol, Eduardo. *Historicismo y Existencialismo.* Mexico: El Colegio de Mexico, 1950.

Ouimette, Victor. *José Ortega y Gasset.* Boston: Twayne Publishers, 1982.

Orringer, Nelson R. "Life as Shipwreck or as Sport in Ortega y Gasset." *Romance Notes* 17 (1976): 70-75.

——. *Nuevas fuentes germánicas de ¿Qué es filosofía? de Ortega.* Madrid: Consejo Superior de Investigaciones, 1984.

——. "Ortega's Dialogue with Heidegger in *What is Philosophy?*" *Ortega y Gasset Centennial/University of New Mexico.* Madrid: José Porrua Turanzas, 1985, pp. 45-56.

——. *Ortega y sus fuentes germánicas.* Madrid: Editorial Gredos, 1979.

Pina Prata, Francisco. *Dialectica da razao*. Lisboa: Edicoes da Revista Filosofía, 1961.

Raley, Harold C. *José Ortega y Gasset: Philosopher of European Unity*. University: University of Alabama Press, 1971.

Ramirez, Santiago. *La filosofía de Ortega y Gasset*. Barcelona: Herder, 1958.

Romanell, Patrick. "Ortega in Mexico." *Journal of the History of Ideas* 21, no. 4 (October-December 1960): 600-608.

Sánchez Villa, José. *Ortega y Gasset, Existentialist: A Critical Study of His Thought and His Sources*. Chicago: Regnery, 1949.

Sharkey, James. "Ortega, Einstein and Perspectivism." *Romance Notes* 12 (1970): 21-25.

Silver, Philip W. *Ortega as Phenomenologist: The Genesis of Meditations on Quixote*. New York: Columbia University Press, 1978.

Tuttle, Howard N. "Algunos puntos de la crítica de Ortega y Gasset a la teoría del Ser de Heidegger." *Revista de Occidente* 108 (Mayo 1990): 61-69.

———. *The Dawn of Historical Reason. The Historicality of Human Existence in the Thought of Dilthey, Heidegger, and Ortega y Gasset*. New York: Peter Lang, 1994.

———. "The Idea of Life in Wilhelm Dilthey and Ortega y Gasset." *Ortega y Gasset Centennial/University of New Mexico*. Madrid: José Porrua Turanzas, 1985, pp. 105-117.

———. "Ortega's Vitalism in Relation to Aspects of *Lebensphilosophie* and Phenomenology." *Southwest Philosophical Studies* 6 (1981): 88-92.

Walsh, W.H. *Introduction to the Philosophy of History*. London: Hutchinson, 1951.

Weintraub, Karl. *The Value of the Individual: Self and Circumstance in Autobiography.* Chicago: University of Chicago Press, 1978.

Weiss, Robert O. "The Leveling Process as a Function of the Masses in the View of Kierkegaard and Ortega y Gasset." *Kentucky Foreign Language Quarterly* 7 (First Quarter 1960): 27-36.

Wohl, Robert. *The Generation of 1914.* Cambridge: Harvard University Press, 1979.